# Getting to the
# Heart of Learning

## Social-Emotional Skills across the Early Childhood Curriculum

**Ellen Booth Church**

**Photography courtesy of Shutterstock Photography ©2014, www.shutterstock.com.**

## Dedication

To my parents and first teachers, Francesca and Norval Church. They taught me not to just teach a subject but to teach the child.

## Bulk Purchase

Gryphon House books are available for special premiums and sales promotions as well as for fund-raising use. Special editions or book excerpts also can be created to specifications. For details, contact the Director of Marketing at Gryphon House.

## Disclaimer

Gryphon House, Inc., cannot be held responsible for damage, mishap, or injury incurred during the use of or because of activities in this book. Appropriate and reasonable caution and adult supervision of children involved in activities and corresponding to the age and capability of each child involved are recommended at all times. Do not leave children unattended at any time. Observe safety and caution at all times.

# Getting to the HEART of Learning

## Social-Emotional Skills across the Early Childhood Curriculum

**ELLEN BOOTH CHURCH**

**Gryphon House, Inc.**
Lewisville, NC

## Copyright

Published by Gryphon House, Inc.

P. O. Box 10, Lewisville, NC 27023

800.638.0928; 877.638.7576 (fax)

Visit us on the web at www.gryphonhouse.com.

## Library of Congress Cataloging-in-Publication Data

Church, Ellen Booth.

  Getting to the heart of learning : social-emotional skills across the early childhood curriculum / by Ellen Booth Church.

     pages cm

Includes bibliographical references and index.

  ISBN 978-0-87659-580-0 (alk. paper)

 1.  Early childhood education--Activity programs. 2.  Social learning.

3.  Emotional intelligence. 4.  Education--Social aspects.  I. Title.

  LB1139.35.A37C476 2014

  372.21--dc23

                                        2014022750

# Table of Contents

# Introduction

All learning is social-emotional learning. Children do not learn skills in isolation but through social connection and interconnection to the real world—their world. It is their curiosity about the world that stimulates their desire to learn and to share what they have learned. We all learn best when we care about what we are learning and whom we are learning it with. Children live their lives with their hearts and minds open and connected. From that union of heart and mind, they develop into people who are balanced, happy, and successful.

Take a quick look at what is being presented in the news, and you will see the need in our culture for social-emotional development. Preschool and kindergarten teachers recognize both the need to address social development in their students and with their students' families and the need to teach the basic skills that are essential to learning. These two things do not need to be separate; in fact, they truly are inseparable. Perhaps the trick is to recognize the connection and emphasize it in our interactions with children. It is one thing to know a concept and another to apply it to everyday life.

## How to Use This Book

Each section—math, science, language, literacy, and motor skills—is designed to offer easy and interesting ways for the children to explore and develop their understandings. The activities list the subject-area skills the children will be learning, as well as the social-emotional skills that they will develop as they work together.

- **Let's Get Involved:** Begin a new topic with engaging circle-time activities. Introduce the concepts that you will explore, and get the children involved and interested. Group involvement builds social skills while creating a broader experience.
- **Let's Explore Together:** Broaden and deepen their explorations with activities designed to lead them to new discoveries. The activities can be done in centers or as large-group explorations and encourage teamwork, communication, sharing, listening, and other social-emotional skills that support children's success in the classroom and beyond.

I think, at a child's birth, if a mother could ask a fairy godmother to endow it with the most useful gift, that gift should be curiosity.

—ELEANOR ROOSEVELT, first lady of the United States, author, and politician

■ **Learning Extensions and Building Community:** Learning is an ongoing process that deepens when children revisit a concept in many different ways. This section provides activities that expand the learning both inside and outside the classroom. Playground and home activities help the children see how to apply the learning to the world around them. Family involvement helps children apply the social skills they are learning in school to their family relationships. And, activities with writing, art, music, and movement help children see the arts in all learning.

This book is much more than an activity book. It connects the reader both to curriculum content and to the deeper meaning of shared activities. Each activity is designed for building academic skills and social-emotional learning. Please join me as we explore some basic understandings and then dive into fun and learning that will create community as well as knowledge.

# All Learning Is Social-Emotional Learning

## CHAPTER 1

Social and emotional learning starts with you. Our own self-awareness is one of the most important ways we can assist children as they grow and learn socially and emotionally. By exploring your own feelings and approaches, you develop an understanding that can help you see how you view and respond to children. Take a few minutes to ask yourself some questions. You might want to explore a question a day. Write your thoughts in a notebook or journal, and revisit them throughout the year.

- How did I feel about school as a young child?
- What was my social style in preschool and kindergarten?
- What were my social challenges and successes in the early years?
- How can I use these memories to build awareness about the children I teach?
- As a teacher, how do I feel about going to school most days?
- What are the challenges of working with young children?
- What are the gifts of working with young children?
- How do I feel my group functions as a community?
- What do I do to build strong and meaningful relationships with my students?
- Do I listen and acknowledge feelings?
- Do I create an environment of trust and support that encourages children to share their feelings? How do I motivate children to solve their own problems?
- Does the classroom environment support individual styles and positive social behaviors?
- How much do we laugh and smile in our class?

# Defining Social-Emotional Learning

If you take a look at recent writings about schools and programs, you will see these three letters: *SEL.* But what is SEL? Why is it so important? SEL is social-emotional learning. Social-emotional learning can be described as the development of the skills children need to understand and manage emotions, become self-aware and self-regulated, develop an understanding of others, create positive relationships, and problem solve.

Studies are showing that children are more able to learn basic academic skills when their social and emotional skills are positive and strong. In fact, a report from the Child Mental Health Foundations and Agencies Network indicates that the key to success in kindergarten and later schooling is not whether children know their ABCs and 123s but the quality of their people skills. Being ready for school means being friendly, confident, cooperative, focused, and curious. This makes sense. Children are more able to concentrate on learning the basic skills if they feel successful, appreciated, and accepted in the group. Think of the young children entering your classroom for the first time. They are navigating a new environment with multiple expectations, rules, and children. Young children need an amazing combination of cognitive, motor, creative, and social-emotional skills to function in a classroom—and that is even before they learn their first letter or number. Often, a classroom full of children is the largest group of other children they have ever encountered. In the early childhood years, children are learning how to be themselves and be a part of a group, how to interpret others' feelings while trying to control their own. Wow!

Early childhood teachers are currently dealing with an increased need to address social and emotional issues in their classrooms. Challenging behaviors such as bullying and violence, which were once associated with older children, are now occurring in the younger children. At the same time, teachers are seeing people-pleasing behaviors and neutrality, which can be indicators of low self-esteem. There are many programs available to focus on and deal with these SEL issues directly. But at the same time, teachers must teach the basic skills in the domains of literacy and language, math, science, creative explorations, and physical development. This book is designed to do both! It helps teachers engage children in activities that will support social-skill development while also reinforcing skills in a variety of other domains. This approach offers ideas to help teachers teach from a viewpoint of creating joy in the classroom: the joy of learning, the joy of interacting, and the joy of being!

# The Research Base

There has been abundant research in the area of social-skill development in preschoolers. One important study, the Tools of the Mind project conducted by Elena Bodrova and Deborah Leong, is based on the work of Lev Vygotsky. Interestingly but not surprisingly, their research supports children's use of their own mental tools, including social and emotional skills, to further develop their cognitive skills.

Similarly, the book *From Neurons to Neighborhoods: The Science of Early Childhood Development,* edited by Jack Shonkoff and Deborah Phillips, cites recent research in early childhood development, underscoring the importance of social-skill development:

> Establishing relationships with other children is one of the major developmental tasks of early childhood. How well children fare at this task appears to matter. It matters to the children themselves, creating a context in which they evaluate their self-worth, competence, and view of the world as pleasant or hostile. It matters to their future, as the patterns of peer interaction in early childhood increasingly predict whether children will walk pathways to competence or deviance in the tasks of middle childhood and adolescence. And it matters to the other children a child comes into contact with, as the experience of children in peer groups depends in good measure on the nature of the other children with whom they interact. Yet playing nicely, making friends, and being a good friend are not all that easy for young children. These tasks confront them with increasing demands on their developing cognitive and emotional capacities.

We can look to recent brain research to see the importance of social-interaction skills. Studies are showing that a child's ability to interact with others, control and express her feelings, and take care of basic self-help tasks independently are as important for success in school as any academic skills. But perhaps most important, research shows that the neural pathways needed for learning are actually constructed through positive interactions with others!

This is not news to early childhood teachers. We have always known the importance of positive interactions with children. However, these studies give us support for what we have seen, felt, and experienced in our wonderful group times and activities with children. All those special projects you share have actually helped prepare the children for learning. Each time you present a shared activity, sit in a group, or create something together, you are helping children make connections with others in the class, to share and care, to listen and speak in a group, and to feel confident when taking on new challenges.

# Great Groups Set the SEL Stage

How many times have you heard an adult tell a child to "use your words" during emotional situations? The problem is that young children often do not have the words to use! Each of the activities in this book starts with a circle time. Circle time is one of the best places to set the stage for social and emotional learning through activities. Perhaps more than any other part of your day, your circle is the place for building community and collectively expressing thoughts and feelings. It takes a number of social skills to be able to just sit, listen, and take turns in a group, making circle time the perfect place to get started for the day. Consider your group time as a microcosm where prosocial awareness and growth can develop. The social dynamics of sharing, listening, taking turns, and respect are practiced every day in your meetings together. By helping children focus on cooperation and collaboration, you will be creating connections that will assist them in working together in the small group activities of this book. In fact, you can introduce each activity at circle time. This way you will be creating a focus not only on academic skills but also on social-emotional learning.

Your group gathering is also a wonderful place to introduce the vocabulary the children need to express feelings and name the social skills they are learning. Here are a few things to consider:

- **Focus on emotions:** Children often can talk about a book character's feelings better than they can talk about their own. Choose books to read that depict characters who are experiencing a particular emotion. Point out the emotion word, and use it in the discussion. For example, you might choose a book with a character who is angry. You might ask, "How is he feeling? How do you know this?" Then invite children to think

about whether they have ever felt the same way. This simple process encourages the children to build a vocabulary of emotions that will help them use their words when a problem arises. You might want to focus on one emotion word a week, using literature, songs, and examples to keep the conversation going.

- **Focus on social skills:** Choose a social-emotional skill word each week to highlight with your group. Then, when you are sharing activities together, you can reinforce the vocabulary and the concept throughout the day. For example, you might want to talk about the word *listen.* An important part of feeling welcome in a group is the feeling of being listened to. Listening skills are essential to social and emotional development and are key to a good circle time together. Consider using reflective listening as a staple of your shared circle. By taking the time to focus on this skill, it will quickly become a natural part of your classroom community. In reflective listening, children are asked to remember and share what they have heard someone say. This is incredibly validating for children. You can model this in circle time by repeating what you heard a child say and asking if you are correct. Then, you can ask others to share as well.

- **Use gerunds to introduce social-emotional concepts:** Gerunds are verbal nouns that end in *ing,* such as *running* or *hopping.* The late, wise, and wonderful early childhood educator Clare Cherry suggests in her book *Please Don't Sit on the Kids* that teachers use gerunds to give simple directions in a positive way. This is a tried-and-true technique that really works. When you want children to remember what they are supposed to be doing, use one gerund as a short-and-sweet reminder of appropriate behavior. This is so much more effective than all the sentences of directions in the world. If, for example, children are not looking at you or listening, you could say, "Looking," or "Listening." Or, when children are running down the hall, you could say, "Walking." The one simple word is easy for children to hear and respond to, is empowering, and builds vocabulary. Plus, a gerund is a positive reminder instead of a big *no* or *do not.*

# Developmental Milestones of Social and Emotional Learning

Children meet social and emotional learning opportunities based on their experiences and their developmental levels. To better understand the ways children respond to these learning opportunities, it is helpful to know children's social-emotional tendencies at each age and stage. This knowledge helps us to have appropriate expectations and to create engaging activities that fit their needs.

> Education is not preparation for life; education is life itself.
> —JOHN DEWEY, American philosopher and educator

## Three-year-olds might:

- appear eager to please but may not always understand the rules;
- be hesitant to join in large-group activities and games;
- not always be willing to take turns and share;
- defend toys, space, and themselves physically with hitting, grabbing, and pushing; or
- observe others in play, play parallel with other children, or join in for short periods of time.

### You can support them by:

- verbalizing, modeling, and reviewing the class rules for clarity and encouragement;
- offering short, simple social-interaction activities that provide an immediate sense of success;
- stopping an activity that is falling apart and positively redirecting them to another activity;
- allowing children to watch large-group activities without pressure to participate;
- finding simple ways for children to participate as a helper or as your partner;
- giving reluctant or disruptive children a job to do during circle time;
- understanding that they may not be able to share easily and providing multiples of toys and options that help children have a sense of success with sharing;
- starting out small and simple by counting out equal numbers of snacks or blocks to use and introducing the word *same* in terms of having the same number of items;

- playing simple turn-taking games and emphasizing turn taking in all activities, such as songs, dances, and board games;

- providing positive options for dealing with conflict by demonstrating actions a child can do to protect himself and his toys; and

- allowing children to find their own play styles while encouraging them to participate with others, such as by modeling interactive play with the children in the dramatic-play area.

## Four-year-olds might:

- look for approval and support from adults and can be overly enthusiastic at times;

- want to be told what to do and be proud of doing so;

- like to help the teacher and sometimes other children but may tattle on other children if they think the rules are not being followed;

- start to use words instead of physical aggression but can be punitive and threatening;

- participate cooperatively in dramatic play, role-playing, and make-believe, and have an imaginary friend; or

- be able to sit and participate in large-group activities for longer periods of time but may still try to monopolize the conversation with exaggerated tales.

### You can support them by:

- providing support that is specific to the behavior you want to encourage, such as telling the child you are proud of the way he is sharing a toy or putting something away;

- ignoring excessive enthusiasm if it is not disruptive to the class;

- encouraging a sense of cooperation among the children by letting them participate in creating class rules;

- inviting the children to share what they know of the class routines and rules;

- recognizing that the children may be very literal about the rules and may tattle for small infractions;

- helping the children understand the difference between tattling and asking for help;

- modeling conflict-resolution skills and providing appropriate words and phrases to use in conflict;

- valuing dramatic-play interactions throughout the day, encouraging make-believe and creative thinking;

- understanding that the children can sit longer in a group but being aware of when they are getting distracted and losing attention; and
- using listening and turn-taking activities to build awareness of sharing the group's attention with others.

## Five-year-olds might:

- cooperate in group activities without needing constant direction;
- follow directions but test the limits and authority of adults;
- enjoy making friends and have a special playmate or best friend;
- have better self-control of emotions and actions but still have difficulty in stressful situations;
- use laughter and comic behavior and words to gain attention and make friends;
- need adult support, attention, and comfort with challenges; or
- recognize other children's feelings and needs.

### You can support them by:

- gradually extending group-activity times by carefully monitoring children's interest and capabilities;
- being aware that the children are developing their individuated selves and will naturally test limits;
- being flexible with the rules and directions to empower the children to begin to take responsibility for themselves and each other;
- understanding that a best friend one day may not be a friend the next day;
- setting up activities that encourage children to play with a wide variety of their classmates;
- watching for children who start to exclude others or create cliques;
- helping children notice when they are using self-control;
- using specific language so that children can understand what behavior it is that you are supporting;
- creating a joyful classroom filled with shared laughter and warmth;
- ignoring and redirecting children who use inappropriate humor to gain attention;
- remembering that, even though children are seemingly more socially and emotionally competent, they are still young children and will come to you for loving support and comfort;
- being the island of support they can return to when they feel challenged by waves of emotion and interaction;

- sharing words for emotions that children can relate to; and
- talking about the feelings and needs of characters in literature as a means for reflection and empathy.

# Sailing the Seven *Cs*: Using Learning Activities to Build Social-Emotional Skills

**A journey of a thousand miles must begin with a single step.**
**—LAO-TZU,**
**Chinese philosopher and poet**

Young children who come to your class are embarking on a voyage of school that could last them more than fourteen years. Along the way, they will meet a variety of children, teachers, and people. How do we prepare children for this journey? We teach them with social and emotional skills that will support them as they learn the content inherent in each level of schooling. We cannot predict everything young children will have to learn by the time they get to high school and college; the world is constantly changing. But one of the constants in the changing journey is the child's ability to be a happy, confident, and contributing member of the group. In the early years, we know that children who have the basic social-interaction skills are ready and able to concentrate on the task of learning academic skills. But a focus on SEL does not mean that children will have rich experiences that lead to reading, writing, and arithmetic. In fact, the approach in this book focuses not only on learning skills in the social and emotional areas but also on the academic realm as well. The activities are designed to invite children to think and problem solve on all levels from social to academic. It is simple: if a child is not able to take turns, listen, and sit in a group, she will struggle to learn what is being taught in the group.

**THE SEVEN Cs OF SOCIAL-EMOTIONAL LEARNING**

Cooperation

Communication

Curiosity

Caring

Contemplation

Confidence

Competence

# Cooperation

As an early childhood teacher, you know the importance of building cooperation skills in your classroom. The activities you plan and the games and songs you use all teach children how to work cooperatively with others. In many ways, any activity you present to your group is a cooperative activity because the children must share, take turns, and listen. You can also choose activities that present even more obvious opportunities to build cooperation skills, helping the children learn how to empathize, work with, and get along with others. It is in the area of cooperation where children's self-regulation skills can be most tested. Through the challenge of working in a group, children learn how to regulate their feelings, behaviors, and attention. From these cooperative experiences, collaboration and great ideas are born. As a four-year-old once asked me, "Can't we all be nice and do it together?"

# Communication

From cooperation comes communication. To truly be a member of a cooperative group, you have to be able to communicate with others. This is an interesting skill to develop in the early years because of the widely divergent language abilities of our children. Some children come to school with a vast vocabulary and are very self-expressive. Others might just look at you with big, wide eyes and say little or nothing! One of the key skills children can learn in your classroom is the ability to express themselves, to communicate and represent their ideas, feelings, and knowledge about the world. By creating an environment of acceptance for all, you send the message that children's voices will be heard and respected. When the children feel comfortable expressing an idea or opinion, they will be more open to learning in all areas of the curriculum. They will be willing to take the risks of thinking and problem solving that build higher-order thinking skills. Communication is an essential skill at the core of all reading, writing, math, and science skills. It is a great gift to be able to communicate ideas!

# Curiosity

Children are naturally curious. The smallest pebble on the sidewalk can open doors of wonder and experimentation in a second. Science, math, art, and language can occur simultaneously in that moment of wonder. But, curiosity is also an important skill for social and emotional learning, because curiosity can help children take a more expanded view of the world around them and all that inhabits it. How many times have you heard a child ask, "Why does she look different? Why does he walk funny?" and similar questions? These curious observations create the right moment to discuss acceptance and understanding of those with similarities and differences. Perhaps one of the most important skills to develop at this age and stage is a true curiosity of learning with each other. Through your small- and large-group activities, children learn to share their curiosity with others. We are always learning from each other!

## Caring

Curiosity can lead to caring, compassion, and empathy. When children notice the similarities and differences among their friends, they also learn to accept that we are not all alike but we all have feelings that can be hurt or helped by our caring interactions. It is amazing to watch children care for a new child in the class or offer to help someone who is struggling. Your shared activities help children to see how to support and actively care for each other. Children learn the joy of helping, listening, and supporting. As children develop out of the egocentric stage, they begin to see themselves as part of a larger whole. Children understand that sharing the world with others is not only a responsibility but also a gift!

## Contemplation

This might seem like an unusual *C* to have in this list for young children, but it is actually a skill that children can learn at a young age. They just need to be encouraged to do it! Contemplation is the art of listening to our hearts and learning how to relax with our interplay with the world. More and more schools are offering opportunities in the day to stop, relax, rest, and reflect. Reflection time does not have to be a formal time. It can be a reminder for children to take a breath and stop before they react or respond to something. The good news is that children love these opportunities to reflect and are becoming more joyful. Plus, teachers are noticing a positive shift in the social and emotional climates of their classrooms. Just by taking a breath, we all can create space in the day that will let the jumbles settle and the clarity arise.

## Confidence

Developing children's senses of confidence and self-esteem are essential. Your interactions help children feel good about their identities both individually and in relationship to others. This is an enduring skill that will help children feel it is safe to express an opinion, try something new, or make a mistake. If children believe in themselves, they will tackle more and more difficult learning challenges in all areas of the curriculum. Confidence helps children develop persistence and resilience. These are all skills that will assist children as they progress through school.

## Competence

The journey brings us to the final *C*: competence. It is where all the others are leading us. Through our warm, nurturing acceptance, children develop confidence in themselves and trust that they are competent to handle the challenges of the world. While competence is related to confidence, it is different. Confidence can be viewed as a child's belief in his abilities. Competence is the child's perceived ease in participating in small- and large-group learning activities. Competence is the shore we are arriving at with a sense of joy in our sails.

# Play Is the Vehicle for the Learning Journey

The activities here are based on interactions with real-world materials and with each other. They are open ended and play based in that they are designed to invite children to express creatively their ideas, thoughts, and feelings. One child's project will not look like another child's. We have heard it said before: play is important work for young children. Many of the skills children are learning in your class are best learned in play situations. Allow children to "mess around" with concepts, apply them to new situations, and construct their own knowledge. Children learn by investigating the world through interacting with it. Our first job as teachers is to set out the materials and concept and watch them engage. But that isn't enough. We also have to be prepared with questions that invite children to think about their play and what they are doing. Through your communications with children, you fortify and honor their play. In the activities, I suggest questions you can ask children to take them deeper into understanding and reflecting about their play. Through sequences of questions and communications, you open the door to higher levels of thinking and build on the children's innate sense of wonder.

So, before you turn the page and read on, take a moment just for you. Rest and imagine you are floating on the sea. Take a deep breath, and smell the salt air. Hear the sounds of gulls and waves. Breathe and know that what you are doing for the welfare of the children really does make a difference. Thank you for your commitment to children.

# Getting to the Heart of Math

## CHAPTER 2

Your math activities—sorting, classifying, patterning, seriating, graphing, counting, and measuring—build the essential social skills of cooperation and sharing. These small- and large-group activities work best with a team and provide children with the opportunities to help each other explore concepts and ideas. The fun of sorting and classifying is heightened when the group works together to explore these concepts in different ways. Patterning is more interesting when someone "reads" your pattern and shares it with you. Measurement often takes a pair: one to hold and the other to measure. Predicting and estimating are more interesting when many people share their guesses! Of course, number work also builds self-confidence as children proudly share their abilities to count objects and recognize numbers. Let's explore math concepts together!

# It's in the Box!

Children love boxes of all shapes and sizes, making boxes the perfect tool for exploring basic math concepts. Children will build math and cooperation skills as they work together to explore sorting, matching, and seriating.

## Materials:

- Boxes in a variety of sizes, some with lids
- Variety of items that will fit into the boxes
- One shoe box
- Red construction or wrapping paper
- Tape
- Small, unbreakable mirror
- Glue
- Whiteboard or chart paper
- Marker
- One appliance box, such as a microwave box

## Ahead of Time:

- Cover the shoe box with red paper.
- Glue the unbreakable mirror to the inside bottom of the red box.
- Fill the big appliance box with many smaller boxes.
- Place the items that fit into the boxes around the room for the children to discover.

## Math Skills:

- Sorting
- Matching
- Seriating

## Social-Emotional Skills:

- Acceptance in the group
- Cooperative thinking
- Playing fair
- Working together

## Let's Get Involved

1. Bring the red box to your circle time. This is bound to pique the children's curiosity and get the group conversation going.

2. Sing the following lyrics to the tune of "The Little Red Box" to welcome the children to circle time. If you do not know the tune, you can make one up, find a version online, or say the words like a poem or chant.

   *Oh, I wish I had a little red box*
   *To put my good friends in.*
   *I'd take them out and X, X, X (blow three kisses)*
   *And put them back again.*

   Tell the children that your magic box has your special friends inside. Ask them if they would like to see.

3. Go around the circle, singing the song for each child and letting the child look inside to see who is in the box. When he looks inside, he will see himself!

4. Talk about boxes. Ask the children, "What can you do with a box? What are boxes good for?" Invite them to cooperatively brainstorm all the different ways to use a box. You may have to give them some ideas to get going. Ask open-ended questions, such as, "If it were a rainy day, how would you use a box?" "What could you do with a box if you needed to build something?" "How do you use boxes in your home?" "How do we use boxes here at school?" Write the children's ideas on chart paper or the whiteboard. Even though children cannot read all

the words, they know their ideas are written there. This is an important validation of both their thinking and their social membership in the group.

## Let's Explore Together

Many of the essential math skills can be presented and developed with boxes. These activities can last quite a while as a focus for your math area that will help the children recognize that math is inherent in the world around them.

1. Start big! Bring a big box filled with smaller boxes to your math area. Ask the children to guess what is inside. They may guess boxes, but they might guess an object based on the size of the box. There are no wrong answers, just happy guesses!

2. Spill out the contents of the box, and encourage the children to freely explore the smaller boxes. This is the "messing around" stage when they need to just touch and experience the boxes. This can be exciting for children, and some grabbing may occur. Reinforce the concept of playing fairly with the objects and with each other. Remind the children that they are sharing the boxes and will soon find out what they are going to do with them.

3. When they have finished this stage, they are ready for a task. Invite the children to work together to sort the boxes into piles. They might want to sort big and little at first. Another day, they could sort by color or by shape.

4. Ask the children to notice the differences between the two piles. Some are very big, and some are very small, but some are in between. Ask, "Can we make three piles: small, medium, and large?" Encourage them to sort the boxes again. If you want to extend this activity, the children can also put the boxes in a line from smallest to largest.

5. Give each child a box, and invite the children to go around the room to find things that fit inside their boxes. Ask them to bring the items back to share and show.

6. On another day, add boxes with lids to the box focus. Let the children practice matching for size and shape. This is a quiet activity that can be comforting for children. They enjoy the repetition of matching the lids over and over again.

7. The children will naturally start building with all these wonderful boxes. Encourage them to explore ways to balance their boxes to create buildings and towers. Invite them to quantify their building: "How many boxes is your tallest tower?" "How many boxes long is your building?" "What is the tallest tower you can make?" Eventually, you can add some of the boxes to your block area.

## Learning Extensions and Building Community

1. Children feel a sense of acceptance in the group when they can offer something from home. Invite families to send in clean boxes, such as empty food, toy, and clothing boxes, which will make great store materials for your dramatic play area. Children will enjoy adding their boxes to the store shelves. Add a small cash box or register, and go shopping!

2. Add art. Invite the children to use boxes to make a shadow-box collage. They can take a walk outside with their chosen box to collect natural items. Back inside, they can glue their found items in the box. Collage materials work well, too.

**SEL SPOTLIGHT**
In the early years, the need for acceptance is paramount. Many children are coming from a home situation where there are few children, and they can be overwhelmed by the number of children they deal with at school. Activities that help children feel accepted and appreciated by the group for their ideas and their actions are key to building a sense of security.

# Pattern with Me!

Patterns are everywhere, but we might not notice them unless we are looking. Let's really look at patterns and use them for building math skills.

## Math Skills:

- Matching
- Patterning
- Noticing

## Social-Emotional Skills:

- Sharing
- Taking turns
- Listening
- Self-esteem

## Materials:

- Large colorful beads
- Strings
- Colorful shape blocks, such as attribute or parquetry blocks
- Cardboard or construction paper
- Scissors
- Patterned fabric strips
- Small trays, placemats, or mats
- Small items for object patterning, such as buttons, small cars, stones, or pinecones

## Ahead of Time:

- Cut out basic shapes—triangle, square, circle—from the construction paper or cardboard.
- Wear something to school that has strong recognizable patterns, such as patterned socks, a scarf, and a patterned skirt.
- Hang some patterns around the room, such as strips of fabric or picture strips.

## Let's Get Involved

1.  At circle time, introduce the concept of patterns all around. Your clothing is a great place to start. Welcome the children with a silly song, sung to the tune of "Twinkle, Twinkle, Little Star":

    *I'm a pattern, can't you see,*
    *From the head and toe of me.*
    *Red and blue and red and blue,*
    *That's my pattern, oh so true.*
    *I'm a pattern, can't you see,*
    *From the head and toe of me.*

    Invite the children to notice the pattern of colors you are wearing. Point to each one as you move from head to toe. They can say it with you: red, blue, red, blue.

2.  Talk about what makes a pattern. A pattern is something that stays the same and repeats over and over again. Explain that this week they are going to be exploring patterns with each other and all around.

3.  Get the children's bodies involved. Often, children understand best if they "do" a pattern. This action is a good opportunity for children to listen in the group. Make a simple AB pattern, such as tap, clap, tap, clap. Ask the children to tap their legs and clap their hands. They may need a bit of time to catch on, but once the rhythm and pattern is in place, they will continue the pattern.

4.  Encourage the children to make AB patterns for others to do. They may need your help at first, but eventually they will catch on to making two repeating movements. There is nothing like the feeling of the other children doing your movements!

## Let's Explore Together

1.  Patterns are important because they are inherent in counting and other number relationships. Start in a small group in your math area using small objects to present simple patterns. For example, make a row of button, stone, button, stone on a mat or tray.

2.  Ask the children to "read" the pattern with you by saying it: button, stone, button, stone.

3.  Ask them to clap the pattern with you. For the button, clap twice, and for the stone, clap once: but-ton, stone, clap-clap, clap.

4.  Ask the children to extend the pattern: button, stone, button, stone, button. What comes next? Encourage them to add more objects to the pattern to match it. Then, read it together again.

5.  Invite the children to take turns making their own two-part AB pattern for the others to "read." They can use the same object or the other objects you have collected.

6.  Introduce the beads or blocks as new materials for pattern making. They can try making a row of two different shapes or colors of blocks, or they can string two different colors of beads in a pattern. Allow the children some exploration time with these new materials before adding the next stage of the activity.

7.  Give the children trays or mats for creating patterns. Place the blocks or beads in front of the children, and explain that you want them to watch your pattern carefully as you make it and then make one just like it on their mats. Encourage them to copy your pattern.

8.  Pair the children, and ask the pairs to sit facing each other. Give each child a mat and some blocks or shapes.

9.  Ask one child in each pair to make a pattern on his mat, and encourage the other child to repeat it. Then, the second child can make a pattern, and the first child can copy it. This may take some help from you at first, but once they understand they will enjoy the challenge.

10. Take the challenge up a notch by doing the patterns back-to-back. Ask the children to sit with their backs together with the materials in front of them. One child can make a pattern and describe it. The other child

can listen to the description and try to copy the pattern. After they are done, they can turn around and see if the patterns match. This is a wonderful opportunity for children to listen to each other.

## Learning Extensions and Building Community

1. Take a walk around the room and look for the patterns you have placed and for any other patterns in the environment. Remember, there are patterns in windowpanes, ceiling tiles, lights, and so on.
2. Walk outside to find patterns in nature, too. Remind the children that they are looking for a pattern that shows colors or shapes or objects that repeat.
3. Expand your patterns. After the children have a sense of repetition in the patterns, they can begin to do more complicated patterns, such as three-part ABC patterns. Eventually, they will be able to recognize and repeat AAB or ABBA patterns! This activity can go on all year!
4. Encourage families to explore patterns at home. They can go on a pattern hunt around the house—the sock drawer is a great place to start—and create their own patterns out of household objects.

**SEL SPOTLIGHT**

Perhaps one of the hardest skills for young children to learn is listening. Listening to a friend can be particularly challenging, because this type of listening is different from listening to a teacher and following directions. Listening to another child takes an understanding that she has something to say and that it feels good to stop and listen. Partner activities that require listening skills are helpful for building this social and emotional skill.

# Is It Time Yet?

Young children are just learning about the concept of time and do not yet have a concept of noon or five o'clock. But, they do understand the pattern and sequence of events in a day. That's a great place to start!

## Materials:

- Photos or drawings of the events of the day*
- 9" x 12" card stock
- Drawing paper
- Crayons and markers
- Digital camera and printer (optional)
- Ribbon or yarn (optional)
- Small photo albums (optional)
- Scissors
- Hole punch
- Glue

## Ahead of Time:

* Create a series of 9" x 12" cards featuring images that represent the sequence of the day. Images might include arrival, circle time, centers, snack, story time, outdoor play, nap, and so on. Free printable symbols are available on www. environments.com.

## Math Skills:

- Sequencing
- Patterning
- Left-to-right progression
- Ordinal numbers

## Social-Emotional Skills:

- Making self-directed choices
- Self-comforting
- Controlling oneself
- Group participation

## Let's Get Involved

How many times have you been asked questions such as, "Is it time to go home yet?" "When is Mommy coming?" "Is it snack time now?" Introduce the sequence of time with experiences and images.

1. Start your circle time with a surprise. You will get the children's attention and cooperation quickly. Pretend to be confused about the time—the more dramatic you are, the better. Say, "Okay, now it's time to go home. I hope you had a fun day today at school. What did you do today? What are you going to do when you go home?" The children will quickly let you know that you are wrong and that, in fact, it is circle time and not the end of the day.

2. Thank them for their help and ask, "How do you know that it is morning?" The children may offer that it is the first part of the day, that they just got here, or that they have not had snack yet. Help the children notice the different ways they knew what time it is. This will help them notice that time is the passage of events.

3. Once you have established that it is morning, you can ask the children to tell you what will happen next: "What do we do after circle time? What happens next?" The children may remember some of the sequence of the day but not all. This is not a test but an opportunity to explore the concepts of time and sequence. Explain that this week they are going to explore time.

## Let's Explore Together

After introducing the concept in the large group, you can work with small groups in your math area. This will give the children some hands-on experiences with sequencing and patterning time.

1. Show the children the sequence-of-the-day cards you have created. Put them out on the table in random order. Ask the children to look at the photos and tell you something about what they see. Use questions to get the conversation started and spark some thinking: "What is happening in this picture?" "What are the children doing? Where are they?"

2. Children will naturally recognize the things they do at school. Invite them to help you organize the pictures from the left side of the table to the right to create a sequence of the day in order. You can ask them to find the first thing they do and put that on the left. They can then look for the next thing. Or, they can find the last event and put that on the right. This is a good way to introduce the words *first* and *last*.

3. Encourage the children to work together to discuss the sequence. It is not important for them to get it exactly right but to develop a sense of progression. Show the children how they can use the pictures to know what is happening next: "This picture shows activity time, but what is next? Yes, clean-up time. Then, what do we do next?" Verbalizing the pattern helps children understand it better.

4. When the cards are placed in sequence, ask a question such as, "Is it time to go home yet?" Encourage the children to find the card for your present activity: "It's activity time now. Let's see how many things we will do before we go home." The children can count along with you as they point to the cards.

5. Make time personal! Let the children make their own *My Day at School* books to keep in the room. These can be an excellent resource for them when they are feeling upset and want to go home. They can check their books to see where they are and where they are going next in the sequence.

   ■ Use a digital camera to take photos of the children in each of the events of the school day. This can be a shortened sequence with the events that are most important to them.

   ■ Print the photos.

■ Let the children put them together in a book showing the sequence of the day's events from arrival to departure. Small dollar-store photo albums work great for this. Alternatively, punch holes in the left-hand side of the pages and let the children tie the pages together with yarn or ribbon to create a book. The children can add their own drawings to create more personalized books.

## Learning Extensions and Building Community

1.  After you have used the cards for the learning activities, find a place in the room to display them in a line from left to right. This provides children with a quick resource to help them decide what time it is and to make a good choice for participation in the routine.

2.  Add a song. Use the tune of "Here We Go 'Round the Mulberry Bush" to sing about the day. You can sing a verse for each section of the day:

    *This is the way we come to school,*
    *Come to school, come to school.*
    *This is the way we come to school*
    *So early in the morning.*

    Continue, adding verses for each event. End with the following:

    *This is the way we go back home,*
    *Go back home, go back home.*
    *This is the way we go back home*
    *So late in the day.*

3.  Share the idea of picture sequence cards with the families. It is a wonderful tool they can use to encourage their children to be more aware of the family day and to take responsibility for the things they can do. Recognizable sequences are comforting to children and can help children feel more secure.

**SEL SPOTLIGHT**
Adults control so much of a young child's life! Of course this is important for a child's safety and learning, but children also need to develop their ability to make good choices and control themselves. Simple visual images and reminders provide children with the tools for making self-directed choices without asking for help.

# The Measure of Me

The concepts of inches and feet are too abstract for young children, but they can understand the process of measuring by using familiar objects and themselves.

## Math Skills:

- Matching
- Measuring
- Estimating

## Social-Emotional Skills:

- Following directions
- Seeking peers as play partners
- Asking for help

## Materials:

- Ruler, yardstick, or tape measure
- Ribbon, thick yarn, or string
- Small items, such as socks, pinecones, blocks, and books
- Whiteboard or chart paper
- Marker
- Construction paper
- Scissors
- Glue or tape

## Ahead of Time:

- Cut a variety of lengths of ribbon, yarn, or string to make measuring strips.
- Cut construction paper into 12" strips.

## Let's Get Involved

This is a fun topic to start in the group and then expand to an exploration of measurement throughout the classroom. Once children get the idea of nonstandard measurement, they will want to do it all the time!

1. Show the children some standard measuring tools such as a ruler, yardstick, and tape measure. Instead of telling them what you have, ask them: "Does anyone know what this is?" "What would someone use it for?" "Do you know anyone who uses a tool like this?" "What are some of the things you have seen someone measure?"

2. Tell the children that almost anything can be a tool for measuring. They do not have to use a ruler to find out how long something is. Propose a group challenge for the children to share. Ask them to guess how many books long the circle-time area is. Listen to their guesses, and record them on the whiteboard or chart paper.

3. Give each child a book. Ask the first child in the circle to put her book at the top of the circle area. The next child adds a book beside the first, and then the next child adds a book. Continue until the area is measured from the top to bottom. Count the books together. Whose guess was close? If there is time, try measuring the circle with a different material such as blocks.

4. Try the nonstandard measuring game several times over many days. The children will enjoy it, and each experience makes their understanding of the measuring process deepen.

## Let's Explore Together

1. Turn your math area into a measurement center. Provide a variety of nonstandard items that can be used for measuring. After you introduce the materials, the children will be able to work independently with them in their own way.

2. Suggest to the children that they can use their hands as measurement tools. This creates a personal connection to the topic. Invite the children to use their hands to measure furniture in the area. The children may need your help in understanding how to do this. Demonstrate measuring with a few children's hands. Do not worry about accuracy in counting and measuring—the process is more important than the product.

3. Ask the children to choose one of the lengths of yarn as their tool. Show them how to hold the yarn up to something and stretch it across. Ask them to go around the room looking for things that are the same size as their tool. If the items are small enough, children can bring them back to the math table to show the others.

4. Children may like to trade measuring tools with someone and try over and over again. It is fun to find the things that match and are the same size. Remind the children that they can ask for help from you or a friend. Sometimes it helps to have someone hold one end while the child holds the other.

5. Use math language to reinforce their work. Besides the word *measuring*, you can talk about *matching, more than,* and *less than.*

6. Ask the children to choose something big that they want to measure. Ask them to estimate how many of their tools long the object will be, then let them measure to find out if their guess is close. Do not worry about accuracy; this is preliminary practice in estimating. The children will enjoy guessing and measuring.

## Learning Extensions and Building Community

1. Let the children work together over time to create a super-long paper chain. Use the chain to measure the room and beyond. Challenge them to make a chain as long as the room or the hall. Take it out on the playground and measure there, too. The children will have to work together and ask for help because the chain is just too big to handle on their own.

2. Invite the children to lie on the floor as you cut a strip of ribbon the same size as they are. Challenge them to find an item that is the same size as their ribbon. The children can keep their ribbons in the math area or their cubbies for easy use.

3. Try tracing the children's feet to create personal "foot rulers" for measuring, too. Make a family connection with this fun activity. This will be a great opportunity for children to show their families what they are doing and to let the children teach them the directions.

**SEL SPOTLIGHT**
Knowing when to ask for help is a tricky skill for young children. Many are accustomed to having a family member around who helps with everything. In a group at school, they need to do things more on their own. You can assist children by helping them to know when to do something for themselves and when to ask for help. When they ask for help with something small that they are capable of trying, invite them to try to help themselves first. When a child is struggling, step in immediately, saying, "I am here to help!" This helps them to begin to know the difference.

# It Takes All Sorts

Sorting and classifying are Math 101 for young children. These important skills are the foundation of understanding basic math facts. Why not explore sorting and classifying with objects that are inviting to see, touch, and hear?

## Materials:

- Pillowcase or cloth shopping bag
- Small items in a variety of sizes, shapes, and textures
- Crayons
- Drawing paper
- Stuffed animal
- Small bag

## Ahead of Time:

- Fill a pillowcase or bag with a variety of objects of different textures. Choose items that are pleasing and comforting to touch.
- Put a single item in a small bag.

## Math Skills:

- Matching
- Sorting
- Classifying
- Comparison
- Graphing

## Social-Emotional Skills:

- Sharing
- Awareness of senses
- Following directions

## Let's Get Involved

Touch is an important sense for children. It can bring great comfort as well useful information. Start this study of sorting and classifying with a game in your circle time, and then extend into the math area.

1. Show the children a stuffed animal from your home, your own toy if possible. Children will be amazed and thrilled to see you have a stuffed animal, too! Introduce your friend and explain how you like to touch it when you are sad or upset. The children may like to carefully pass the toy around. Tell them they can take three touches and then pass to the next child.

2. Ask the children if they have a special stuffed animal to hold at home. Listen as they tell you about their stuffed-animal friends.

3. Introduce a guessing game to take the concept of touch further. Put one object in a small bag, and go around the circle asking the children to reach inside and touch it with their fingers. Sing the following song to the tune of "Row, Row, Row Your Boat":

*Touch, touch, touch your hand*
*Right inside the bag.*
*Gently, gently, gently, gently*
*What's inside my bag?*

4. Invite the children to both describe how the object feels and guess what it could be. Do not show it until everyone has had a chance to touch and guess. Note: Some children will be uncomfortable with reaching in the bag. Allow them to watch the game. They may join in at another time.

5. Invite reflection by asking questions: "Did you like how the object in the bag felt? How did it make you feel when you touched it?" Listen to the children's responses. Explain that this week they will be exploring how things feel and the different ways we can sort them.

## Let's Explore Together

In the math area, show the children how to use touch and texture to sort and classify things.

1. Place your pillowcase or bag filled with items in the center of the math table. Invite a small group to join you in exploring the contents in many different ways. You can repeat the song for circle time while playing the game.

2. Ask the first child to reach inside the bag and touch something. Ask, "How does it feel?" "What could it be?" Introduce vocabulary to describe the textures of the different items, such as *bumpy, smooth, hard, soft, squishy, furry,* and so on. Encourage the child to show what she found in the bag.

3. Move to the next child and repeat the process, going around the table until the bag is empty.

4. Inspect the objects for sorting and classifying. Use words for texture as you sort together. This will expand the understanding and deepen the awareness of the differences used in classifying: "Let's put all the fluffy things in one pile, the bumpy things in another, and the smooth things in a pile, too."

5. Look at the objects in many different ways to build flexibility of thought. Move on to sorting by size or color: "Which items are similar in color? Let's put them together in one pile. Let's see how many different piles we can make."

6. Invite the children to notice how many by asking them to guess which pile is the biggest and which is the smallest. Count and see!

7. Graph it! Encourage the children to create rows out of the items in each pile. Start each pile at one end of the table and build up. This will make it even easier to see which pile has more or less than the other.

On another day, try it again another way. The children can make piles sorting by shape, size, or whatever you like.

## Learning Extensions and Building Community

1. Young children can easily learn the art of making rubbings of textured materials. Show the children how to put a piece of paper on top of an object and gently rub with the side of the crayon to create a wave of color. The texture of the object will show through on the paper!

2. Walk with me. This activity works with just two children at a time and with plenty of supervision, but it is such a marvelous opportunity for children to work together with trust and care that it is worth the extra effort. You might want to invite a helper to come to class when you do this activity. One child closes his eyes. The other child carefully takes him by the hand, bringing him to different things to touch in the classroom. Once children get used to the idea, they will love it!

3. Ask the children to bring in an object from home that they like to touch. It must be something that is safe and that the family says is okay to bring to school. The children can then share their special touch friends with the group. Look at all of the items together and ask, "How many ways can we sort them?"

**SEL SPOTLIGHT**

There is a great deal of sensory input in any given early childhood classroom. A soft corner in the classroom can be a good place for children to rest and be calm. But, some children need more activity. They may need to bang on clay or build with blocks to get out some feelings. It is important to have a multisensory setting that meets the needs of all children.

# We Are Quite a Pair

Sorting and classifying can be a beautifully endless topic of study for young children. Each time you revisit it with a new focus, you expand the children's understanding and the application of the knowledge to themselves and their world.

### Math Skills:

- Matching
- Counting
- Graphing

### Social-Emotional Skills:

- Finding a partner
- Sharing
- Noticing change

### Materials:

- Pairs of familiar items, such as socks, shoes, and gloves
- Sets of matching toys, such as small cars, animals, and dolls
- 9" x 12" pieces of card stock or cardboard, enough for each child to have two
- Small blocks in different colors, sizes, and shapes
- Drawing paper
- Crayons and markers
- Large bag or basket

### Ahead of Time:

Prepare two sets of large 9" x 12" number cards on cardboard. Draw the numeral *1* on the front of one set, and add one dot at the bottom as a cue. On the other set draw the numeral *2* on the front, and add two dots at the bottom as a cue. Make enough for each child to have a set.

## Let's Get Involved

When you think about it, there is a great deal needed to understand the concept of *pairs*. Not only do children need to understand there are two things, but that these two things go together for some reason.

1. For a little fun and novelty, come to circle time overly dressed in pairs! You can wear a pair of crazy socks and shoes and silly gloves or mittens. This will get the conversation started.

2. Start the meeting as you always do, without bringing any attention to your attire. The children are bound to notice the change and speak about it. Noticing change is an important social skill that helps children become aware of their environment and react appropriately. Ask the children to describe what they are noticing.

3. Draw the conversation to the pairs of things you are wearing: "Yes, I have on a pair of silly shoes! I'm wearing a pair of silly socks and gloves, too. How many shoes am I wearing? One, two. A pair is two!"

4. Invite the children to notice where you are wearing the pairs of things. You need two parts of your body to wear the shoes, socks, and gloves. Ask the children to look at their own bodies to find some pairs: "Can you find your pair of hands? Hold them up! What else can you find? Show us."

5. Celebrate the discovery of pairs with a little rhyme the children can say and act out:

*One, two, I've got two.*
*My ears, my eyes, my hands, my shoes.*
*One, two makes a pair.*
*Pairs are one plus one makes two.*

6. Play a pairs movement game for finding a partner. Have the children stand and make two circles, one inside the other. As you lead the children in saying the rhyme, the circles walk around in different directions. When the rhyme is finished, the children stop, turn, and face a partner.

7. Begin saying the rhyme. When the rhyme is finished, ask the children to turn and face their partner. Tell them, "You are a pair." Ask them to shake hands, and have them point to the pairs of body parts they have. Call out, "Ears, eyes, hands," and so on. Have them shake hands and start again.

## Let's Explore Together

Once the children are introduced to the concept of pairs, they will become more aware of them in their own bodies and in the world around them. These activities can be done over time to deepen the experience of matching pairs and counting by twos.

1. Bring a small group together in your math area. Remind the children of the topic by saying the rhyme again and asking them to find pairs on their bodies: "Pairs are two things that are alike. What do you have two of?" Children often start with hands and feet. Show the number cards with the numerals 1 and 2: "One, two makes a pair."

2. Let the children choose a partner. A fun, easy way to choose a partner is for each child to take a number card from a pile. A child who has a number 1 pairs with a child who has a number 2. Provide drawing papers and crayons for tracing each other's foot or hand. One child traces while the other holds still, then they switch. The children can then decorate their drawings and cut them out. Ask the children to notice how their pairs match. These can later become a part of a bulletin board display of pairs.

3. Set out a large bag or basket of matching materials on the math table. Invite the children to empty the contents and make pairs with the items

inside. Some will be easy at first, but provide some challenging items as well. For example, you can have cars or toys that are similar but not actually matching. This will help children expand their understanding that sometimes a pair is just two things that are similar. Use the number cards to match pairs of things. One item goes on the 1 card and the other on the 2 card.

4. Use the table to create a graph. Have the children organize their pairs in rows of two starting at one end of the table. Count them: one, two. Ask, "How many pairs of two did we make?"

## Learning Extensions and Building Community

1. Children love to see themselves represented on the walls of the classroom. Create a pairs bulletin board to display the feet and hand pairs of the class.

2. Sing "The Hokey Pokey," to bring the children's attention to the pairs on their bodies:

    *You put your pair of hands in,*
    *You put your pair of hands out.*
    *You put your pair of hands in,*
    *And you shake 'em all about.*
    *You do the Hokey Pokey,*
    *And you turn yourself around.*
    *That's what it's all about!*

    Continue singing, adding their knees, elbows, heels, hips, and so on.

3. Practice pairing with a partner during transitions. Pass out the number cards upside down so children cannot see the number. Count to two, and ask them to turn the cards over to see their numbers. Then, they can find their partners.

**SEL SPOTLIGHT**
Throughout school, children will have to find a partner many times. This sounds like a simple task, but for many it is a real social and emotional challenge. A shy or reticent child often cannot take the first steps, and the bossy child can take over. Activities that focus on selecting partners help children become more comfortable with this process that they will need for a long time to come.

# Square It Up!

## Materials:

- Construction paper in a variety of colors
- Scissors
- Blocks in a variety of shapes and sizes, such as parquetry or attribute blocks
- Square items such as books, pillows, or pans
- Drawing paper
- Glue sticks
- Sticky notes
- Cardboard (optional)
- Craft sticks (optional)

## Ahead of Time:

- Cut the basic shapes—circle, square, rectangle, and triangle—out of sticky-note paper, with enough for pairs of children to have one of each shape.
- Cut a variety of the basic shapes in different sizes out of construction paper.
- Cut the drawing paper into 5" x 12" strips.

**Optional:** Make a shape viewer for playing Shape I Spy. Cut an outline of a square out of cardboard, and attach it to a craft stick.

Shapes are all around us, and young children are just beginning to notice the differences among them. Many children come to preschool already knowing the names of many shapes, but they need experiences that go beyond naming. Hands-on experiences with using shapes for sorting, patterning, graphing, and measuring provide children with the practical understanding of how shapes function in their world.

## Math Skills:

- Shape recognition
- Same and different
- Estimating
- Sorting
- Patterning

## Social-Emotional Skills:

- Waiting
- Cooperative thinking
- Participating in a group
- Sharing in front of a group

## Let's Get Involved

1. Welcome the children with a song sung to the tune of "Do You Know the Muffin Man?" Hold up a shape, and sing the song:

   *Do you know what shape this is?*
   *What shape this is?*
   *What shape this is?*
   *Do you know what shape this is?*
   *Tell me, tell me, please.*

   Count to three, then ask, "What is it? Shout it out!" Encourage the children to wait until the song is finished and you have counted to three before they say the answer together.

2. Use the song to go through all the basic shapes of circle, square, rectangle, and triangle.

3. Place a few square objects in front of the group. You might choose books, blocks, pillows, baking pans, or paper shapes. Invite the children to notice what is the same and what is different about these things. You may have to help them recognize that the objects are all squares. Ask,

"What is it that makes them all squares?" Lead them to the discovery that each item has four even sides.

4. Talk about the shapes that are in the room. If you choose, you can use shape viewers to focus children's attention on a particular shape. Play Shape I Spy, focusing on squares: "I spy with my little viewer something that is square like my viewer. Who sees something?" Encourage the children to take turns looking around the room for something that is square. Other days, you can focus on a different shape in the room using the song and additional viewers.

## Let's Explore Together

Continue the focus on shapes in your math area with a variety of matching, sorting, and patterning activities. Each time you provide a new experience with a familiar shape, the child's brain connects prior understanding to new information.

1. Put the shape blocks or paper shapes in a pile in the center of the table. Invite the children to take a handful and spread the items out on the table in front of them.

2. Ask, "What shapes did you grab? How are they the same or different?" Encourage them to talk about the shapes they have in their piles.

3. Invite the children to explore the shapes they scooped up by sorting them into different piles.

4. Pair the children, and ask each pair to put their shapes into a common pile. Encourage them to sort the shapes again with their partners.

5. Ask the pairs to estimate how many shapes they can pick up. One child scoops and the other counts. Young children are not good at estimation yet, but practice is essential. Each time they guess how many, they get closer to an understanding.

6. Invite the pairs to look for matches in the shapes. Encourage them to sort by shape then by color.

7. Go on a shape hunt together around the room. Give pairs of children a collection of the shape stickers you made out of sticky notes. Encourage them to work with their partners to find a shape in the room that matches the sticker and to place the shape sticker on that item.

8. At the end of the hunt, encourage the children to take turns showing what shapes they found. They can go around and point out all their stickers. Ask them to count how many shapes they found. This type of

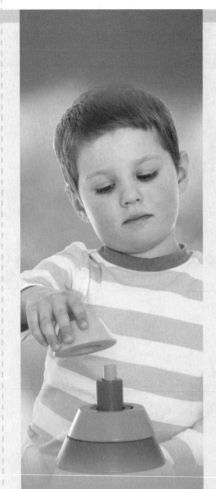

sharing with the group is an important way for children to feel that their work is seen and respected.

9. Graph the hunt. Ask the children to collect their stickers and bring them back to the table for another activity. Place a construction-paper square, circle, triangle, and rectangle at the top of the table. Encourage the children to place the stickers in columns of shapes on the table. Start at the bottom and work to the top. This makes it easier for children to count and see how many of a shape they have found.

10. Give children strips of drawing paper, and encourage them to create simple patterns with their shapes. They can start with two shapes that repeat, then eventually add more.

## Learning Extensions and Building Community

1. Make shape art. Children can experiment with the paper shapes to make mosaic pictures and can add decorations with crayons.

2. Offer a fun challenge by showing children how they can use safety scissors to cut a square in half "point to point" to make two triangles. Children are fascinated by this and will do it over and over again! Encourage them to use the shapes to make pictures or other shapes.

**SEL SPOTLIGHT**

Each time a child shares something that she did or something that she knows with a group, she builds a sense of belonging. The process of having others watch and listen to her sharing validates her thinking and her identity as a contributing member of the group.

# Graph Alert!

Graphing is an essential problem-solving tool for organizing information and thinking. It is the important next step that helps children understand sorting and classifying symbolically.

## Math Skills:

- Same and different
- Graphing
- Quantifying
- Comparing
- Representing

## Social-Emotional Skills:

- Cooperating
- Sharing with a group

## Materials:

- 9" x 12" card stock
- Images of a variety of people
- Recorded music
- Crayons
- Clean shower-curtain liner (optional)
- Painter's tape (optional)
- Stickers
- Chart paper
- Markers
- Tempera paint
- Liquid dish detergent
- Paintbrushes
- White glue
- Small milk cartons (optional)

## Ahead of Time:

- Make people graphing cards: On 9" x 12" sheets of card stock, draw or glue images for categories of people and features, such as boy, girl, short hair, and long hair; and colors, such as red, blue, green, and so on.
- Tape the people graphing cards along the wall in your movement area. On the floor in front of each card, put a piece of painter's tape to show the children where to stand.
- Make a graphing mat: Use a clean shower-curtain liner and colored tape to make a grid pattern of boxes that are approximately six inches wide. Children can use this over and over again for making graphs of real items.
- Prepare the milk cartons: Wash them thoroughly. When they are dry, push in the tops of the cartons so that each forms a cube.

## Let's Get Involved

Jean Piaget taught that young children in the pre-operational stage are searching for representation and are learning how to use symbols as a means of doing this. Let's start with a fun group game at circle time to focus on graphing.

1. Play Musical Graphs! Show the children the boy and girl people graphing cards on the wall in the movement area. Ask the children to

guess what the cards might say. Talk about what each card symbolizes. Tell them you will play music and let them dance around. When the music stops, they are to move to the sign that fits them. For example, if a child is a girl, she can stand in front of the girl card. Boys can stand in front of the boy card.

2.  Play some music and allow the children some free-movement time. Stop the music, and remind them to move to stand in their category.

3.  When children have moved to the cards, have them look to see what they have created—a graph! Ask, "How many boys are in our class?" "How many girls today?"

4.  Continue the game, expanding the categories to long hair and short hair or to the colors the children are wearing.

## Let's Explore Together

Any sorting and classifying activity can become a graph when you use real objects. Start with comparing two groups, and then move on to graphing more.

1.  Start with something simple, practical, and available, such as crayons. Ask the children to help you sort out the crayon box. They can sort the crayons in two piles: broken and unbroken.

2.  When they have created the piles, ask, "How do you know which we have more of? Let's graph it." Have the children make two lines of crayons side-by-side on a piece of paper or a graphing mat. Count the crayons and see which group has more.

3.  This graph needs a bit more cooperation from the group, but it also helps children share more in the activity. Ask the children to look at their shoes. What do they notice? How are their shoes the same or different from a friend's shoes? Invite each child to take off one shoe for better comparing. The children can put the sneakers in one pile and the other kinds of shoes in another pile. Ask, "How many do we have of each?

4.  If available, stretch a graphing mat out for children to use. Choose a category for each column. Ask the children to take turns putting their shoes in the appropriate column. Which do you have more of, sneakers or other kinds of shoes?

5.  Graph again another way. This time, have them put the shoes on the graphing mat according to the shoe color. Which color shoe do you have the most of? Try tie shoes versus non-tie shoes, too. Each time

you take the same material and change the way of looking at it, you expand children's understanding.

6. Introduce the idea of voting graphs. Choose a fun topic such as their favorite ice-cream flavor, food, cartoon, song, or game. You can use stickers for each category for children to paste in the appropriate column, or you can simply ask each child to make a check mark with a marker in the appropriate column. All the chocolate-ice-cream lovers vote in one column, and the vanilla or strawberry lovers in the others. What flavor wins the vote? This is a great way to learn more about the community and to learn how to use representational graphs.

## Learning Extensions and Building Community

1. Have the children make their own graphing cubes. Give the children the milk cartons you have prepared. Let them paint their cubes using tempera paint mixed with a little liquid dish detergent. (This will allow the tempera to stick to the waxy surface of the cube.) After the cubes are dry, have the children paste their photos or personal symbols on one face of the cube. They can use their cubes in graphing situations when a child can vote for choices or preferences.

2. Extend the movement graphs to include other topics. For example, for the topic of animals and where they live, the categories could be land, sea, and air. On the wall, place signs and pictures representing the three categories. To play, the children can hold toy animals and move around like their animals. When the music stops, they can move to the sign representing where their animal lives. Then, they can trade animals with someone else and do it again. You can adapt this activity to fit any theme you present.

3. Introduce the concepts of *more than* and *less than* with graphs. Each time you compare a line in the graph, invite the children to notice which column has more and which has less. They can also count how many more or fewer.

**SEL SPOTLIGHT**
Some activities take more cooperation than others. Creating a good blend between cooperative large-group games and small-group activities helps children learn the nuances of cooperating in different situations. At this stage, most children are better at cooperating in small groups. Challenge them with fun large-group activities that are so motivating to play that they will want to cooperate!

# It's in the Balance!

Pan balance scales were once an integral part of any early childhood math and science area, but they are getting harder to find. Here are two simple ways to work with balance and weight using handmade tools.

### Math Skills:

- Balancing
- Estimating
- Weighing

### Social-Emotional Skills:

- Sharing
- Moving with a partner
- Cooperative brainstorming

### Materials:

- String
- Plastic clothes hanger
- 2 plastic cups
- Hole punch
- Scissors
- 10–12 small cans, sharp edges covered in duct tape
- Playdough
- 10–12 long, narrow boxes (Lorna Doone or Petit Écolier cookie boxes work well)
- Small materials such as dried beans, pom-poms, and foam peanuts
- Counting cubes or math counters
- 2 plastic grocery bags
- Sand
- Butcher paper or mural paper
- Paintbrushes
- Glue
- Pillows in a variety of sizes (optional)
- Playground ball
- Rope

### Ahead of Time:

Make a simple hanging balance scale. Gather a plastic clothes hanger, two plastic cups, a hole punch, scissors, and string. Punch holes in the edges of each cup in three equidistant places. Cut six 10-inch lengths of string. Tie a piece of string through each hole. Tie one cup to each hip of the hanger to make a hanging scale.

## Let's Get Involved

Start the focus in your circle time with some fun balance games. This will give children the physical sensation of balancing.

1. Welcome the children with a song and a game. Sing a balancing song to the tune of "I'm a Little Teapot." After you demonstrate the song, invite the children to stand and join you in rocking and balancing. Children may want to repeat this song several times.

   *I'm a little seesaw—see me rock!*
   *Back and forth and forth and back*
   *When I get all balanced, see me stay.*
   *No rocking is for me today!*

2. Talk about how it feels to rock back and forth. Did they feel like they might fall down if they rocked too far? How does it feel to stop and stay balanced?

3. Ask the children to be sure they have enough space around them so they do not bump into someone else. Invite them to use their bodies to experience balancing.

   - Ask them to try balancing on two knees.
   - Ask them to balance on two feet, then on one foot.
   - Ask them to try to balance on two feet and one hand.
   - Ask them to balance with a friend.

   Try a wide variety of challenges that give children the experience of being in and out of balance.

4. Play a partners rocking balance game. Invite the children to find a partner and sit face-to-face with legs crossed. Reach out and hold hands. Now one person rocks forward while the other rocks back. Ask children to rock back and forth, noticing what happens when they rock too far. Sing the see-saw song as they play.

## Let's Explore Together

1. Introduce the children to the concept of balancing on a scale using different balances. They will understand the process of balancing better if they participate in the making of a scale. Pair the children, and provide each pair with a can; a lump of playdough; and a long, narrow box.

2. Show the children how to gently place the side of the can on the piece of playdough. Then, challenge them to find a way to balance the box on the can. At first, the children may try random placements, but eventually they will discover the importance of centering the box on the can.

3. Provide dried beans, pom-poms, counters, packing peanuts, and cubes. Ask the children to try to balance two piles of items on the box. The children will find that not only do they have to watch how much they put on the each side of the box, but also they must watch where they place the items. Do not worry about trying to teach anything now. Allow some great experimentation time with the materials and concept.

4. Introduce the hanging balance (or a pan balance, if you have one). Ask the children what they think will happen to the balance when you put some beans in one cup. Listen to their predictions.

5. Put some beans in one cup. Ask the children what they notice. Ask, "How can we make it balance? What can we do with the other side?" Listen to their ideas.

6. Invite the children to experiment with slowly putting one item at a time in the cups. If the children fill the cups too fast, everything will spill right out!

7. Encourage the children to try balancing a variety of objects in the classroom. Invite them to estimate how many of one item will balance with a number of another type of item. Encourage them to test their guesses with the balance.

8. A pendulum is a fascinating tool for observing balance and flow. Ask the children to help you fill a plastic grocery bag with sand. Tie the top handles together, and attach a string through the top. Hold or hang the bag over the math table.

9. Invite the children to experiment with swinging the bag back and forth. What happens if it goes too far? What happens when they stop pushing?

10. Put a large piece of mural paper on the table below the pendulum. Using paintbrushes, brush some glue on the paper. Let the children poke a tiny hole in the bottom of the bag at the middle. Gently push the bag, and watch the sand come out and make a picture!

## Learning Extensions and Building Community

1. There is something special about playing with pillows. They are easy to use and nobody gets hurt! Bring in a stack of pillows for experimenting with balance. Encourage the children to work together to build a tower of pillows. At first, they may not realize that the large ones need to be on the bottom and the smaller ones on top. Allow them the fun of trying it different ways and giggling when it all falls down. Eventually you can step in and show them the importance of making a base.

2. Extend the balance to the playground by making a pendulum ball game. Place a ball in a plastic grocery bag, and tie a rope through the bag's handles. Hang the bag in an open area under a tree or climber, low enough that the bag almost touches the ground. Invite the children to experiment with moving the ball back and forth. What happens when they stop pushing it? Place some lightweight objects under the bag. Let the children experiment with knocking the items down with the pendulum.

# Count Me In

Young children are thrilled when they learn how to count to ten! But, often they just know the words and do not know how to count to an object. They need experience with counting objects to develop an understanding of what the numbers mean.

## Math Skills:

- One-to-one correspondence
- Counting
- Beginning adding
- Beginning subtracting

## Social-Emotional Skills:

- Participating in routines
- Seeing themselves as members of the group
- Concern for others

## Materials:

- Cardboard
- Fabric squares or library pockets
- Glue
- Permanent marker
- Index cards
- Basket
- Paper lunch bags, one per child
- Math counters or buttons
- 4–5 muffin tins
- Construction paper
- Glue
- Pennies
- Small ball
- Animal crackers
- Bowls
- 2 large plastic tubs
- Water or sand
- Scoops or shovels
- Paper
- Crayons
- Paper strips (optional)

## Ahead of Time:

- Make an attendance board. Glue library pockets or fabric squares to a large piece of cardboard. Write each child's name on a pocket. Draw smiley faces on index cards so that the faces will be visible when the card is placed in a pocket. Place the cards in a basket next to the board. When the children come to class, they can put smiley-face cards in their pockets to show that they are present.
- Write a number from 1–10 on an index card, and draw that number of dots on the card. Make sets of numeral-and-dot cards for the numbers 1–10. Make a set for each child, and put each set in a lunch bag.

## Let's Get Involved

1. Counting is a great way to take attendance and to welcome each child. Try a counting game using your attendance board. Have the children help you count how many smiles they see on the board.

2. Ask the children to count how many children are in the circle. Start at one end of the circle and go around. Do not worry if they get messed up along the way. The process is what this is all about. Do the number of smiley faces and the number of children in the circle match? If so, they have one-to-one correspondence! Explain that this week you will be playing many different kinds of counting games.

3. Using the traditional hot-potato rhyme, pass a ball around the circle.

*One potato, two potato, three potato, four.*
*Five potato, six potato, seven potato, more.*

When the group says *more,* the child holding the ball says his name. Play again and again so that all the children get to say their names and to be seen and heard.

## Let's Explore Together

Counting objects can be fun when the materials are fun and interesting. The good news is almost anything can become a counting tool.

1. Give each child a paper bag filled with a set of number-and-dot cards and some pennies, buttons, or counters.

2. Ask them to reach inside their bags, take out a card, and count out a matching number of pennies, buttons, or counters. The pennies are very motivating!

3. Pair the children, and give each pair a muffin tin and some buttons. Provide glue and construction paper, as well.

4. Encourage them to work together to use the muffin tin as they divide the pile of buttons between them. One for you and one for me!

5. Let the children glue their buttons onto construction paper to create a picture.

6. Put animal crackers in bowls for the children to use in a game. Ask them to pretend that the bowl is a zoo.

7. Tell the children that the animals in the zoo want to go exploring. Ask, "Can you help them?" Ask them to carefully reach in the zoo and pick out two animals to hold in their hands. Ask, "How many do you have?" Let them answer you: two.

8. Explain that the animals want more animals to explore with them. Ask the children to find two more animals to hold in their hands. Ask, "Now, how many do you have?" Let them count and answer: four.

9. Tell the children that now one of the animals must go back to the zoo. Ask them to take one away—and eat it if they like! Ask, "Now, how many do you have left?" Let them count and answer: three.

10. Continue the game adding and subtracting the animals until all are eaten!

## Learning Extensions and Building Community

1. Take counting outside on a hot day with a game with water or sand. Fill a big container with water or sand. Put out another empty container for children to use to estimate, count, and fill. Provide smaller containers or scoops for children to use to fill the empty container. Also, consider providing a piece of paper and a crayon to use for tallying.

2. Ask, "How many scoops do you think it will take to fill this empty container?" Let the children guess. Challenge them to fill up the container with water or sand, counting as they scoop. It is helpful to have a piece of paper nearby so that one child can make a mark for each scoop they make. Then, the children can count the marks at the end.

3. Children look forward to a birthday or a special holiday and often get anxious about it. Let a child create a paper chain to help her count down to an anticipated event. Each link in the chain will represent one day. Hang the chain in the room, and at the end of each day, have the child remove one link. Ask, "How many more days until your birthday?"

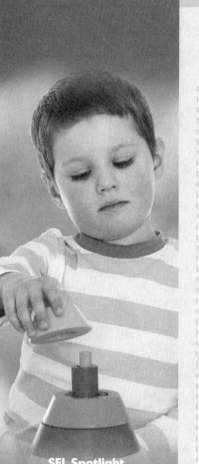

**SEL Spotlight**
Studies show that one of the key factors to success in school is a sense of belonging in the group. In a society that is more and more disjointed, this social and emotional skill is an essential part of the early childhood experience. Your circle time and small-group activities that celebrate children's participation help them to feel recognized and present.

# Getting to the Heart of Science

## CHAPTER 3

Children are natural scientists. They wonder, predict, and experiment with everything! Scientists work best in a lab team, and these activities are designed just for team explorations. The children will explore science themes as well as processes together as they build the social skills of cooperation, helping, and working with others. Many of these activities work best with a partner. The children will have to wait to use materials, control impulses to take over, and communicate ideas together. In the process, children also will be building problem-solving skills that will last a lifetime.

# The Sounds Around

Young children are no strangers to sound! In this activity, the children will explore the sounds in their environments as well as the sounds they make.

| **Science Skills:** | **Social-Emotional Skills:** | **Materials:** |
|---|---|---|
| ■ Listening | ■ Listening | ■ Objects that make different sounds, such as bells, horns, clickers, and so on |
| ■ Observing | ■ Calming behaviors | ■ Paper lunch bags |
| ■ Experimenting | ■ Learning how my senses affect me | ■ Clean paper tubes, such as paper towel and wrapping paper sizes |
| | ■ Making myself heard in a group | ■ Mural or butcher paper |
| | | ■ Crayons |
| | | ■ Masking tape |

## Let's Get Involved

Children use their sense of hearing to help them notice and learn about their world. Working with sound brings in science, listening, and thinking skills.

1. Start the sound explorations with a simple listening game at your circle time. Choose an item that makes an interesting sound, and hide it in a paper bag. Invite the children to guess what is in the bag just by hearing the sound. Listen to all the ideas, and then show them what it is. The children may like to touch and see the object when it comes out.

2. Ask the children to be silent for a few seconds. This will be surprising to them. Ask them to listen to what they can hear in the silence.

3. Ask them what they heard. The children can suggest the sounds in the room, the hall, outside, or whatever they hear. Ask, "How did it feel to stop talking and doing and just rest in silence for a minute?" Talk about the sounds you heard around the room. Ask the children to describe the sounds and how they felt. Did some sounds feel good and make them want to hear that sound again? Which ones? Did other sounds not feel good, making them not want to hear that sound again? Which ones? Explain that they are going to be exploring the sounds around as well as making sounds this week.

> **Note that some children are particularly sensitive to sound, and some sounds will be uncomfortable for them. Be caring and supportive of the child who seems easily disturbed by sound. Allow him to put his hands over his ears if that makes him more comfortable.**

## Let's Explore Together

Surprisingly, a focus on sound can help create a sense of calm in the classroom and the group. By focusing on the sound, children also focus their minds, stop, wait, and listen.

1. Start with a sound hunt. Give each child in a small group a paper lunch bag for collecting items around the room that make a sound. Children can touch the object to hear the sound it makes. For example, you have to shake a set of measuring spoons to make a sound. When children have completed their sound hunt, they can come back to the science table to show and share their findings.

2. Help them understand the variety of sounds by asking them to sort their finds into groups: wood, plastic, metal, and fabric items. Ask the children to notice how some materials make louder or softer sounds. Ask, "Which makes the loudest sound?" "Which makes the softest sound?"

3. Bring the exploration into a personal and physical experience by taking a sound break. Invite the children to experiment with making sounds with their voices or bodies. Ask, "Can you make a soft sound? a quiet sound? a loud sound?" Making a sound in a group can be challenging for some children. Allow some to listen to the others if they prefer.

4. Sound travels through air. Tubes of all different sizes are helpful for exploring this. Put out a collection of paper tubes for the children to experiment with. Encourage them to make a sound with an object, and let another child listen to the sound with and without the tube. How does the sound change? What happens with different size tubes? Is it easier to hear with a short tube or a long one?

5. Extend the sound-tube activity by allowing the children to take the tubes to the playground to explore the sounds outside. A change in venue helps children apply a skill they have learned in one setting to a new setting. This builds understanding and brain connections.

6. Play a call-and-response sound game by making a simple sound and asking them to repeat it. This will encourage the children to listen carefully and work to replicate your sound. Change the mood, the beat, or the volume to encourage the children to experiment with making a wide variety of sounds.

7. End the study of sound back in your circle-time area with a calming and centering activity. Explain that today for story time, instead of reading a book, you are going to tell a story. But, the trick is they have to keep

their eyes closed! Ask the children to find a place to stretch out on their backs to listen to the story. This works best with an unfamiliar or made-up story. Use a calm, clear, and relaxing voice. With their eyes closed, the children will be able to use their imaginations to create the visual images to accompany your words.

## Learning Extensions and Building Community

1. Great artists have often used music to inspire their paintings. Choose a variety of different musical sounds to inspire your budding mural artists to draw. Tape mural paper on the floor in an open area. Invite the children to close their eyes as you play some music. Give the children crayons to draw with. Challenge them to draw with their eyes closed as they let the music move their hands. Periodically stop the music, have the children freeze, and change to music with a different feeling. Ask, "How does your hand want to draw now?" In the end, have the children open their eyes to see their amazing sound mural.

2. Involve the families by sending home sound homework. Give each family a paper lunch bag with the instructions to go on a sound hunt in their home for something that makes an interesting sound. They can shake the item, roll it, blow on it—whatever makes a sound. The children can share their mystery sounds at school in a circle-time guessing game.

# Magnetic You and Me!

What child does not love playing with magnets? Magnetism is an important basic science concept that children can learn and explore with paint and everyday objects. Best of all, the end product is a fascinating piece of shared art. Through cooperatively predicting and experimenting, children build important problem solving skills.

- A collection of metallic and nonmetallic objects, such as nuts, bolts, paper clips, keys, plastic blocks, paper, and buttons
- Pipe cleaners
- Newsprint paper
- Tempera paint
- Water
- Thin plastic trays or plates
- Tape
- Large and small magnets
- Paper or plastic cups

### Science Skills:

- Observing
- Comparing
- Predicting
- Problem solving
- Creative expression

### Social-Emotional Skills:

- Taking turns
- Problem solving
- Expressing ideas
- Supporting each other
- Asking for help

### Ahead of Time:

Wrap one end of a pipe cleaner on each of a collection of metallic objects. This will create a handle for easy dipping in the paint.

## Let's Get Involved

When you introduce the activity in circle time, you encourage the class to work collectively as a group. Group time spent brainstorming and exploring the basic concept of magnets allows the hands-on activity to be a much fuller experience.

1. Place several metal and nonmetal objects in the center of your circle-time area. Use a large magnet for the demonstration and the song.

2. Sing the following song to the tune of "I'm a Little Teapot" to gather the children and create a sense of cooperative interest and group involvement. As you sing, touch the magnet to the metal and nonmetal items.

   *I'm a little magnet, this is me.*
   *Many things will stick to me.*
   *When I touch some metal, you will see.*
   *They stick and stick all over me!*

3. Encourage turn taking by asking the children to share the magnet you used for the song. Start at one end of the circle, and have the children try one object they think will be picked up by the magnet. Then they can pass the magnet to the next person. Continue around the circle.

4.  After everyone has had a try, ask the children to share what they noticed. What items were easily attracted to the magnet? What items were not at all? Do not worry about getting detailed or even accurate answers. The idea is for them to do some cooperative science thinking together.

## Let's Explore Together

1.  On a table, show the children your collection of small items, and ask them to sort the objects into two piles: those they think will be attracted to the magnet and those they think will not be attracted. As they work, talk with them about their predictions: "I see that you have the buttons in the 'won't stick' pile."

2.  Use art to test their predictions. Pair the children and give each pair some tape, newsprint paper, and a thin plastic tray or plate. Have the children help each other tape the piece of paper onto the tray or plate.

3.  Give the pairs a magnet, and let the children select a few objects to test with the magnets. They can place the objects to test on the paper-covered tray. Then, one child holds the tray up so that the other child can easily put the magnet under the tray and move it around. Ask the children to notice if the magnet moves the object on the tray. As they work, reinforce the children's good supporting and helping skills by pointing out clearly how they are helping: "I like the way you are holding the tray low enough for Tom to reach it."

4.  Give each pair of children a cup of tempera paint thinned with a little water. Give them some metallic objects wrapped with pipe cleaners. The pipe cleaners provide a handle for dipping the objects in the paint. Show them how to dip an object in the paint and then set it on the paper-covered tray. They can then move the magnet under the tray to make the metallic object move on top of the tray. Once children have a concept of how this works, they will enjoy freely moving the attracted objects around the paper to create a design.

5.  Allow the children plenty of time to mess around with this concept. It is such fun for them to discover that some objects will move and thus create an artistic line, while others will not. Children may like to take turns holding the plate so everyone gets to draw! Which objects does the magnet move? Which stay still?

## Learning Extensions and Building Community

1. Hide objects in the sand table, and let the children use magnets to search for the ones that will be attracted to the magnets. This is a good way to test and extend their understanding of magnets.

2. Pass out some magnets for the children to use to investigate the classroom environment and find things to which a magnet is attracted. Ask what they notice about the objects that are attracted to the magnet. You also might want to invite the children to find where magnets are used in the classroom. Perhaps there is a magnetic bulletin board or some magnets on the door of the refrigerator!

3. Send home inexpensive magnetic parts holders, found in most hardware stores. These flat dishes are designed to hold metal parts for mechanics, and they make a great base for exploring magnetic art. They will also hold pipe cleaners! Cut a variety of lengths of pipe cleaners for families to use to work together and explore creating designs on the magnetic dishes.

**SEL SPOTLIGHT**
Activities that work best when we help each other are perfect for letting children see how good it feels to help and support a friend. They find out how much fun it is, too!

# You Can't See Me!

Young children love the idea of hiding in plain sight like animals do. In this simple and fun activity, children explore the ways animals hide for protection and safety. This is an activity that can go on for weeks!

**Science Skills:**

- Observing
- Comparing
- Experimenting

**Social-Emotional Skills:**

- Participating in a group
- Waiting
- Following directions

**Materials:**

- Construction paper in a variety of colors
- Scissors
- Tape
- Ziplock or paper bags
- Colored scarves or fabric pieces
- Pairs of objects in a variety of colors
- Photos of camouflaged animals

**Ahead of Time:**

- Cut the construction paper into strips.
- Hide some objects on their matching colors around the room; for example, hide a red block on a red book.

## Let's Get Involved

This is a wonderful topic to explore first in the large group. Children will get a basic introduction to the topic that will help them with the activity to follow, plus they have to use the social skills of following directions and waiting that are essential to all learning activities.

1. Bring several scarves or fabric pieces to circle time. You can use a scarf that matches your clothing or hair to hide behind or under as you sing these words to the tune of "Frère Jacques":

   *You can't see me,*
   *You can't see me.*
   *If you look, do you see?*
   *Hiding in plain sight,*
   *Hiding in plain sight.*
   *I'm right here. I'm right here.*

   This is a "do it again" kind of song. Repetition is a subtle way to invite group participation. The children may like for you to sing the song several times as you pop out of the scarf at the end of each verse!

2. After singing the song several times, invite the children to play, too. This is a wonderful time to teach the children to follow the directions for the song. Ask who wants to try, and let them choose a scarf that matches what they are wearing. Tell them they will hide behind it and pop out at the end! Remind the children to wait for their turn to hide, but reassure them that everyone will get a turn.

3. Talk about the way animals use color to hide. If possible, show photos of animals hiding on protective colorings. There can be a bird in a

tree, but you cannot see it because it matches the branch. If an animal is very still, you will not be able see it. This is called camouflage. *DK Readers: Animal Hide and Seek* by Penny Smith, *Hide and Seek* by the National Geographic Society, and *Where in the Wild? Camouflaged Creatures Concealed…and Revealed* by David Schwartz are great books to use for this activity.

## Let's Explore Together

Gather a small group of children together to explore the concept of camouflage with a fun game.

1. Remind the children of the song and game you played in circle time. You can even sing it again. Children may like to share the directions with the group. Explain that you are going to play a new game and go on an animal camouflage hunt together! Show the duplicates of the objects you have hidden around the room. Tell the children that the objects are hidden around the room on their matching colors.

2. Let each child choose one object to take with him as he looks around the room to find the one in hiding that matches it. Tell them that the trick is to look for places that are the same color as the object. When they find an object, tell them to leave it where it is and just remember where they saw it. Then they can come back to the table. They can help each other, too! Note: Some children will have trouble following the direction, "Do not take it." They often get so excited that they want to bring the object they found to you. Just gently reinforce the directions and rules of the game.

3. Once the children have found their missing items, they can take turns showing the others the hiding places.

4. Extend the game and the understanding by giving children strips of construction paper to hide in places that match the paper color. You can send out two children at a time while the others hide their eyes. Ready or not, let's go find them!

5. When you gather the children back at the table, discuss the photos of animals in their protective-coloring hiding places. They will now be ready to understand how.and why animals do this. Repeat the game as many times as you hold children's interest, then invite a new group to play!

## Learning Extensions and Building Community

1. Take the activity out to the playground. Ahead of time, hide strips of construction paper on their matching colors: browns and greens on natural places, reds and blues on the play equipment, and so on. When the children return with their "finds," they can use tape or a stapler to help you put the strips together for a super-long paper chain. Look how many we found!

2. If you have a nature area to explore, take an animal camouflage walk to see if the children can find any bugs or birds hiding.

3. Prepare bags of colored strips to send home along with a note that gives step-by-step directions for playing as a family. This is a simple game to play at home that will encourage the children to share what they have learned and the directions for the game. It is always a hit!

**SEL SPOTLIGHT**

Children's enthusiasm can make it challenging for them to follow directions. Of course, enthusiasm is a good thing that we want to support; however, as children enter school they need to learn how to listen to directions, wait their turn, and give others a chance. Not always easy to do. Be understanding of children's impulses as well as clear about your expectation that they follow directions. Repeat directions several times before starting. You can even ask the children to tell you what the directions are before you start.

# Waiting for the Sun

The effects of sunlight are all around us. In this fascinating activity, children get to be solar scientists as they observe how the sun can create patterns by fading construction paper. The gift and the trick to this project is patience—learning how to wait.

**Science Skills:**

- Observing
- Comparing
- Brainstorming
- Creative thinking

**Social-Emotional Skills:**

- Waiting
- Sharing
- Helping

**Materials:**

- Unbreakable, powerful flashlight
- Dark-colored construction paper (blue, green, and purple work best—not black)
- Classroom objects and toys with distinctive shapes, such as puzzle pieces, building toys, scissors, paper clips, keys, and so on
- Faded papers or cloth (A good source is the background on your bulletin board!)
- Strips of oak tag or card stock in different widths and lengths (optional)

**Ahead of Time:**

Before you do the Let's Explore Together activity, set out the construction paper and the objects and toys on a table.

## Let's Get Involved

The group can help you take apart an old bulletin board display in your circle-time area. It makes a perfect introduction to the concept of fading.

1. Invite the children to help remove things from the old bulletin board. (Be sure all the items are safe to handle.) "I noticed that it's time to change our bulletin-board display. Can you be helpers and help me take pieces down?" Talk about helping as the children assist you.

2. When all things are removed, draw their attention to the places where the paper is darker and lighter. Help them notice how the shape of the removed object matches the darker imprint on the paper. Ask, "What happened to the paper? What could have caused the paper to fade in one place but stay dark in another?" Listen to their explanations for how that could have happened.

3. Explain that the warmth and light of the sun has the ability to fade colors. If possible, invite the children to find a sunbeam in the room. Ask, "What happens if you put your hand in the sunlight? How does it feel? How is it different from the shade?" "Yes, it feels warm. In a strong light you can see the light through your hand!"

## Let's Explore Together

1. Bring a small group of children to a table where you have set up the materials. Ask the children to remember what they noticed when they

took items off the bulletin board. Let them tell you what they remember about the paper being faded.

2. Explain that this is both a science and an art project. They are going to make a picture without paint or crayons—the sun is going to do all the work. They have to have patience while they wait for the sun to do it, and the sun works very slowly. Take a moment to talk about waiting. Ask the children to suggest what they think is hard to wait for. Maybe it is dinner when they are hungry or a turn in a game.

3. Explain that they will be arranging objects on the construction paper to make a design and then placing it in the sun to fade it. Let each child choose an interesting object to place on a piece of construction paper. Encourage them to suggest what shape the object will create on the paper.

4. Ask the children to explore the classroom to find the place where the sunlight comes in the strongest. Let them arrange their objects on the paper to create a pattern or picture in that spot. Note: Interestingly, black paper does not work well with this activity. It is too saturated with color and takes a very long time to fade.

5. Now the hard part: The children have to wait for several days or a week to see the sun's artful work appear. This is a wonderful opportunity every day to talk about waiting. Encourage the children to carefully check on their pictures' progress each day. Eventually they will have a faded background with the object silhouetted on it.</NL>

## Learning Extensions and Building Community

1. Take a walk around the school to look for other examples of fading. Perhaps you can see curtains or signs that have faded. Invite the children to notice where the sunlight is coming from to create the faded effect.

2. Try it with nature! Take the children for a walk to collect interesting leaves, twigs, and rocks that they can use as the objects for solar-powered art on the playground. Let them experiment with setting a found object on construction paper and leaving it outside on a sunny day. Check it in the afternoon. What happens?

3. The children may like to cut geometric and free-form shapes out of oak tag or card stock to create their own personalized solar art designs. Older children can cut out the letters of their names.

4. Extend the learning and the opportunity to practice waiting with a flashlight exploration. Bring a powerful flashlight to the science area, and ask pairs of children to share the light as they explore the question, "What will the light shine through?" They will have to be careful and take turns as they explore holding different objects up to the light. Ask, "Will the light shine through your hand? Will it shine through a leaf or a block?" Remind them to keep the light away from friends' faces.

**SEL SPOTLIGHT**
Do you ever wonder how many times a day children are told to wait? They may have to wait to get to school, to take a turn in the bathroom, to share a toy, or to wash their hands. First school years are filled with opportunities to learn how to wait. Just naming what they are doing as *waiting* can be a simple and wonderful reminder to do just that. Gently say, "Waiting," to a child who is interrupting or trying to take a turn out of order. You can also let them know that you understand it can be hard to wait, but we all have to do it.

# I'm Melting!

Children are fascinated by change, and melting is particularly interesting! In this activity, children will work together to explore ice and to make predictions.

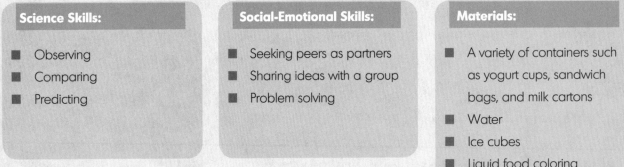

**Science Skills:**

- Observing
- Comparing
- Predicting

**Social-Emotional Skills:**

- Seeking peers as partners
- Sharing ideas with a group
- Problem solving

**Materials:**

- A variety of containers such as yogurt cups, sandwich bags, and milk cartons
- Water
- Ice cubes
- Liquid food coloring
- Scarf
- Box of table salt
- Absorbent paper such as coffee filters, paper towels, or blotter paper
- Magnifiers
- Trays or pans
- Powdered tempera paint
- Craft sticks
- Ice-cube trays

## Let's Get Involved

Most children have had an experience with melting ice, whether it was in their glass or on the sidewalk.

1. Place a big chunk of ice or several ice cubes on a tray, and bring it to circle time. Hide it under a scarf, and play a guessing game. Sing the following song to the tune of "Twinkle, Twinkle, Little Star":

   *There is something under here*
   *That is wet and very cold.*
   *If you step, please beware!*
   *You could slip and fall right there.*

2. Ask the children to guess what is under the scarf. Explain that, just as the song says, this is something that is really cold. They may want to touch the cloth. Listen to their guesses. When someone guesses ice, reveal what is on the tray.

3. Invite the children to talk about what they know about ice. Perhaps they have observed ice melting in a drink or on the sidewalk.

4. Ask the children to notice what has happened to the ice cube on the tray over time: It melted! Why? How? What does the puddle look like? Explain that today they will get to choose a partner to do some ice discovery together in the science art area.

**Ahead of Time:**

- Invite the children to help you freeze a variety of containers filled with water.
- Just before the Let's Explore Together activities, place the ice, trays, food coloring, salt, and absorbent paper in the science center.

## Let's Explore Together

1. In the science center, welcome the small group of "ice scientists" to your project. Talk a little bit about what scientists do. For example, they work together in labs to observe and experiment with new ideas. Ask the children to choose a lab partner to work with.

2. Have each team choose a block of ice, a tray, and absorbent paper to do their study. Ask them to place the paper on the tray and the ice block on top.

3. Ask the children to explore their ice block together. Ask questions to guide their explorations such as, "How does it feel?" "Can you see through it?" "Is it changing?"

4. Propose a prediction challenge. Ask, "What do you think would happen if we put some salt in one or two places on the ice?" Listen to their predictions.

5. Pass the salt container around, and make sure each child gets a chance to sprinkle a little salt on the ice.

6. The children may notice that the salt is starting to melt the ice. Holes will begin to appear. Pass out an unbreakable magnifier for each lab pair to share. Encourage them to take turns looking closely at the changes that are happening.

7. Use open-ended questions to keep the group thinking: "What do you notice about the ice now? How has it changed?" The children will begin to notice that the salt is creating caverns in the ice.

8. Give each team liquid food coloring, and let them gently squeeze drops of food coloring in the caverns or on top of the ice blocks.

9. Make more predictions together: "What will happen to the food coloring? What will the colors do?" The colors will slide down through the cracks in the ice and eventually mix to make new colors, creating a painting on the paper below!

10. Stand back and watch the ice melt. The children may like to go off and do another activity in a different learning center and come and check their ice periodically. They will be learning the scientific process of observation over time.

Encourage the children to raise their hands when they have an idea to share. Have you ever noticed that young children will continue to shout out an idea even when they have their hands raised? A simple trick is to have the children raise one hand while they place the index finger of their other hand over their mouth. It makes a great reminder, and it works!

## Learning Extensions and Building Community

1.  When their ice paintings have dried, invite the children to show their paintings to friends and describe how they made them. This important step helps children learn to verbalize their discoveries and share with the group.

2.  Children can do a smaller version of the activity by painting with powdered tempera paint mixed with water and frozen in ice-cube trays. Place craft sticks in the trays before freezing, to create handles. What happens when the colors meet?

3.  Take it outside—where better to experiment with ice blocks? Let them take their colored ice to the playground or sandbox to notice the puddles they create. Which one is the biggest? Why?

**SEL SPOTLIGHT**

Some young children are very gregarious and can easily choose a partner. Others stand back and watch and hope to get picked. Reinforce the process of choosing a partner frequently by asking children to do this in a variety of settings. For some it is easier when choosing is teacher supported; for others it is easier on their own. Caringly and without pressure, guide children to each other if they need help. One child might like to just stand by and watch instead of choosing. This is just fine. Eventually the watcher will become the doer.

# The Weather Station

Weather is a great subject of study and source of routine for children. It happens every day! You may already talk about the weather, but with this activity children will become more involved in the reporting and can visually see the progression of weather over time.

## Science Skills:

- Observing
- Predicting
- Brainstorming

## Social-Emotional Skills:

- Participating in routines
- Helping
- Focusing
- Listening

## Let's Get Involved

1. Introduce the activity at your circle-time area. Place the large open calendar at the children's eye level. Ask, "What do you think this is? What can we do with it?" Tell them that this is different from a regular calendar because you will not use it to talk about the name of the day or even the date. This calendar is for keeping track of the weather.

2. Invite the children to help you add the weather station to the morning routine: "I need your help. I was watching the weather on television and thinking that we could have a weather station, too. Can you help me? Let's work together to do this."

3. Ask the children to help you decide how to make your own weather station. Ask, "What does a weather reporter do? Can we do that too?" The children may suggest that a weather reporter tells you what the weather is for the day. Encourage the children to help you and each other by adding ideas to how they can observe the weather and report it to the class. Remind the children to listen to each person's idea before suggesting their own.

4. Look outside or take a short walk, and talk about the weather. Encourage the children to describe what they see in different ways. If it is cloudy, is the temperature cold or hot? Is it windy, too? What else do they notice?

## Materials:

- Large blank calendar (can be homemade)
- Large-square graph paper
- Picture symbols for weather: sun, cloud, umbrella, snowflake*
- Construction paper
- Crayons and markers

## Ahead of Time:

- Prepare a weather calendar for your circle-time area. The calendar should have large, open squares to provide room for the children to place a weather symbol each day.
- Prepare a large graph for recording the weather each day for a month. If primary graph paper is not available, make your own by drawing a square grid of one-inch boxes over an entire piece of construction paper. Place one of the weather symbols at the base of each column. The children will color in the space in the appropriate column when they report the weather.

  * Free printable symbols are available on www.environments.com.

5.  Back inside, show the children how to paste a symbol for the weather in the square on the calendar that represents the day: "Today is sunny. Let's find our sun symbol."

6.  Explain that you are going to add a job of weather reporter to the morning routine. The children will take turns being the reporter each day. Post a list of names near the calendar so the children will know whose turn it is each day.

7.  Sing the following song to the tune of "I'm a Little Teapot":

    *I report the weather for today.*
    *Let me look, see, and say.*
    *Today it is raining, I can see.*
    *Drips are falling down to me.*

## Let's Explore Together

This is an activity that builds over time in your circle time. Start with the above introduction, and then continue over many days. Eventually the children will have a collection of weather information recorded in a variety of ways.

1.  Remind the children about the new addition to their morning-meeting routine. Ask them what has been added and how to use it. Adding a weather discussion to the sequence may take some adjustment for the children at first. Each time you add something to the routine, you challenge the children to expand their participation and their understanding of cooperation.

2.  Direct the children's attention to the calendar and the list of weather reporters. Ask, "Whose turn is it today?" The day's weather observer can report her observations and place the correct symbol for the weather in a box on the calendar. Sing the song together, and listen to the weather report. "What does everyone think? Is it sunny today? Yes!"

3.  Ask the children to notice the symbols on the calendar. What do they see? Have there been many sunny days this week? The reporter can ask the group to help count the number of sunny days this week. Any clouds, rain, or snow? Count them, too.

4.  Continue developing this routine by adding a weather graph. This is a very visual and concrete way to record their findings. Each time you add a symbol to the calendar, color in a square on the graph. Eventually you will have rows of squares filled in for the month, making it easy for

the children to see the number of sunny, cloudy, and rainy days. Ask, "Which do we have more of?" "Which do we have less of?"

## Learning Extensions and Building Community

1. Add another element to the routine: a prediction center! At the end of the day, invite the day's weather reporter to think about what the weather will be like tomorrow. Children often see reporters do this on television, so they may be aware of this process and how inaccurate it can be. Anything goes! If you like, you can create a chart for the week or the month. Ask the reporter to place another weather symbol in the prediction center for review tomorrow.

2. Create a big class weather-reporting book. Over time you will have an amazing collection of weather graphs for the different months. The children can work together to make the charts into a big weather book that will be fun to share at circle time. What do they notice about the weather in September as compared to January?

3. Children often like a hat or badge to wear to denote their role for the day. Make one for the class weather reporter! This builds self-awareness and focus.

**SEL SPOTLIGHT**
There is something so comforting about routines for young children. They know what to expect and rest in the familiarity of the routine. But, we also know from brain research that we need to change things periodically by adding novelty. Changing the routine is essential for brain building and social competence.

# Clouds and Me

Young children are often curious about clouds. Clouds come in all sizes, colors, and shapes and make a wonderful medium for scientific creative thinking. While clouds may seem like a distant topic to explore with children, they are actually a constant that preschool children are becoming very aware of. Expand your exploration of weather with a focus on clouds and the feelings they engender.

### Science Skills:

- Observing
- Predicting
- Creative thinking

### Social-Emotional Skills:

- Expressing an idea
- Expressing emotions

### Materials:

- Water table or 2 plastic tubs
- Water
- Sponges of different sizes and textures
- Cotton balls
- Photos of a variety of clouds, such as white, puffy, dark, wispy, and so on
- Straws
- Drawing paper
- Watercolor paints
- Crayons and markers

## Let's Get Involved

1. Start the conversation in your circle time. Be dramatic—be a cloud! "I am feeling kind of cloudy today. I almost forgot to pack my lunch. Maybe I have clouds in my head! Do you ever feel like you have clouds in your head? Let's talk about clouds!"

2. Show the children photos of a variety of clouds. Encourage them to talk about what they notice. They may notice that some clouds are light and puffy and others are heavy and dark. Encourage the children to suggest all the differences they see in the cloud formations.

3. Interestingly, clouds can suggest emotions to children. Show a cloud, and ask the children how it "feels." It might be a happy cloud or a shy cloud or an angry cloud. Often, it is easier for children to talk about emotions with an object than with themselves. "Do you ever feel like a happy cloud floating around the sky? Do you have days when you are a heavy, angry cloud?"

4. Introduce the concept that clouds can bring the weather. Sometimes it is a light, sunny day, and sometimes it is raining. The clouds change all the time, just like our feelings. Explain that this week they are going to experiment with clouds together.

## Let's Explore Together

Create a cloud center in your science area, and over time expand your exploration of clouds to writing and art.

1. Set up two tubs of water in the science area. Talk with the children about clouds and the water cycle. Use dry sponges to represent light, puffy clouds. Invite the children to squeeze and feel the dry sponges. Ask, "How do they feel? Are they light or heavy?"

2. Suggest that they dip their sponges in the water. Ask them to predict what will happen to the sponges when they put them in the water. "How will the sponge feel? Let's try it!"

3. Allow the children plenty of messing-around time with this. They will be fascinated with the changes in the weight, shape, and color of the sponges.

4. Of course, they will also discover that sponges drip when they get really soaked. This is the perfect time to talk about rain! Explain that clouds work the same way. When clouds get filled with water, they start to drip, and that makes rain. Encourage them to make rain together.

5. Expand the activity by changing one variable in the experiment: Add cotton balls. Ask the children to suggest what will happen if they float the cotton balls on top of the water. At first, the cotton balls will float, but eventually they will get heavy and sink. As the children pick them up out of the water, they will discover that the cotton balls drip like rain, too!

6. Clouds can move, too—they just need the wind. Extend the exploration by adding straws. Using dry cotton balls to represent clouds, invite the children to try different ways to move the clouds from one end of the table to the other. They can blow on them, fan them, or use a straw. Interestingly, the straw works best on the side of the cloud, not on top. Allow the children to discover this.

7. Provide watercolors and paper for the children to paint their cloud experience. They may like to paint light, puffy clouds or dark, rainy ones. Encourage the children to explore their feelings as they paint: "How does your cloud feel today?"

## Learning Extensions and Building Community

1. Take the cloud activity outdoors! There is nothing like observing the clouds together. The children may like to stretch out on the ground and

look up to see the shapes and feelings in the clouds overhead. Invite the children to tell you what they see in the clouds: "What do they look like?" "How do they feel?" There are no wrong answers!

2. Make a class book of clouds. The children can use a digital camera to record the clouds over a period of time. Download and print the images, and add them to a photo album. As you look at the photos with the children, ask, "How are the clouds different on a cloudy or sunny day?" "How do you think they feel?" It can be difficult for children to discuss their feelings, but a book of cloud photos can be handy for children to use. They can point to a cloud that best describes how they are feeling today. Over time, you can help the children add more detailed words for the emotions.

3. Toward the end of this study, invite the children to do some cooperative, scientific creative thinking. Ask the children an open-ended question without expecting a right answer. For example, invite them to wonder and share their ideas about where the clouds come from. Accept all their answers equally and with an open mind.

**SEL SPOTLIGHT**

Children are usually pretty good at expressing an emotion but not as strong in labeling it. Often if you ask a child how he feels, he will answer with *good* or *bad*. This is a start, but it is important for children to begin to develop an emotional vocabulary that they can use to help others know how they can help them. Hands-on activities help children explore the words for feelings in a safe environment.

# Mirror, Mirror, Reflect

Young children are fascinated by their reflections and all the different ways to create a reflection. The science of mirrors can also provide an opportunity for self-awareness. This is a topic that can go on for days!

**Materials:**

- Unbreakable mirrors in a variety of sizes
- Aluminum foil
- Unbreakable flashlights
- Masking tape
- Recorded music

**Ahead of Time:**

Before the Let's Explore Together activity, place a variety of unbreakable mirrors in the science area.

**Science Skills:**

- Observing
- Comparing
- Experimenting

**Social-Emotional Skills:**

- Sharing expressions
- Developing self-awareness
- Pausing
- Calming oneself

## Let's Get Involved

1. Bring an unbreakable mirror to your circle. Tell the children, "I brought my mirror from home to share with you. It's the most amazing thing. When I look in it, I see me looking back. If I make a funny face, it makes it back to me. If I make a sad face, it shows me that, too!" Explain that this is called a *reflection*. The mirror reflects or shows just what is there in front of it.

2. Go around the circle, holding up the mirror for each child to look into. Encourage them to experiment with a face or two!

3. Play a simple mirror game with partners. Ask the children to stand and make two circles, one on the inside of the other. As you play some music, ask the two circles to walk in opposite directions: one to the right, and one to the left. When the music stops, ask them to pause and turn to face someone in the other circle. The child in the inner circle makes a movement or a face, and the child on the outer circle reflects it by doing the same thing. Repeat, letting the children have the fun of mirroring each other.

4. Come back to a large circle, and talk about the game. Ask, "What did it feel like to have someone reflect and do what you do?" Listen to the children's descriptions. Explain that this week you are going to be exploring mirrors, reflections, and expressions.

## Let's Explore Together

1. Take a few children on a reflection walk around the classroom. Invite them to look for places where they can see their reflections. They might see them in the windows or door, on appliances, on metal toys, in the water table or sink, and of course in mirrors.

2. Emphasize the word *reflection* each time the children find one. Encourage them to manipulate the images of the reflections by changing their positions, movement, or expressions.

3. Bring the children back to the science table where you have provided a variety of unbreakable mirrors for them to explore. Give them plenty of time to explore the different mirrors thoroughly. They may want to try holding a mirror up to an object to see what it does or putting two mirrors in front of each other. What do they notice? Create an experience chart of the children's mirror discoveries. This can be shared later in a circle time with the whole group.

4. Show the children what can happen if they tape two similarly sized mirrors together. Tape two mirrors together at one side to create a hinged *V* shape. Stand the mirrors on the table with the hinge to the back, and have the children experiment with putting different objects in between the hinged mirrors. What do they see?

5. Extend the mirror exploration with aluminum foil. Invite the children to wrap blocks, books, toys, or almost anything in the classroom with foil. Turn down or turn off the lights, and turn on the flashlights! Let the children explore the reflective surfaces they have created. Encourage them to experiment with the light and the foil to see the variety of reflections they produce.

6. Time to explore their own reflections. Ask the children to try holding a mirror in different positions, such as in front of their faces, then open and close their mouths. They can try holding a mirror at arm's length and up high or down low. Allow plenty of time for the children to explore their own bodies and reflections with their mirrors. Ask them to try slowly moving the mirror to one side or the other then pause and notice what they see from the new angle.

7. Extend the activity of exploring reflections and expressions by using mirrors to draw self-portraits. The children can enjoy looking at themselves in a mirror as they draw themselves on paper. This close looking provides another, deeper level of self-awareness.

## Learning Extensions and Building Community

1.  Take a mirror for a walk! The children will enjoy discovering how to hold a mirror in a doorway while standing inside. What can they see? What happens when they hold a mirror up above their heads or over their shoulders? What can they see behind them? Look in the mirror at the trees and buildings outside. What do they notice that you have not seen before?

2.  Make a shining skyscraper city in the block area. Have the children wrap blocks in foil and then use the blocks to build a city. The children can explore the city with their flashlights. For a special teacher-directed event, add a strip of LED white lights (cool to the touch) to decorate the city. Turn off the classroom lights, and sit and reflect together in the glow.

3.  Interestingly, mirrors can be quite calming for children. Sitting quietly with a mirror allows children a pause to reflect. It may be just what they need on a tough day.

4.  The children might like to write a bit about the self-portraits they created with the mirrors. They can dictate a few words or sentences or a whole story. Put these together in a class book of reflective images. Add an aluminum-foil mirror to the cover of the book. This is bound to be a popular book for reflection in your library.

**SEL SPOTLIGHT**
Children do not stop or pause very often; they are on the go most of the time. But, it is an important social and emotional skill to learn how to stop and notice. When we ask children to notice something such as a reflection, if only for a few seconds, we are providing them with the reason and means to pause.

# A Sandy Solution

If you put sand in front of children, the first thing they want to do is touch it, move it, and make it flow. As a basic element, sand is a wonderful material to explore, both scientifically and socially. Its moving and changeable nature is fascinating to explore with a partner.

## Science Skills:

- Observing
- Predicting
- Experimenting

## Social-Emotional Skills:

- Moving with confidence
- Learning about my body
- Moving with others

## Ahead of Time:

- Before the Let's Explore Together activities, pour dry sand into a variety of containers and set them out in the science area. Set out colanders, sieves, Styrofoam plates, cups, slotted and solid spoons, and funnels as well.
- Before the extension activities, mix dry sand and dry tempera paint in cups. Set out the paint-sand mixture, cotton swabs, white glue in small cups, and drawing paper in the art area.

## Materials:

- Clean play sand
- A variety of containers
- Colanders and sieves
- Slotted and solid spoons
- Funnels
- Heavy Styrofoam plates
- Sand-filled hourglass or egg timer
- Clear plastic cup
- Sharp, pointed tool (adult use only)
- Water
- Pan balance
- Chart paper (optional)
- Marker (optional)
- Egg cartons
- Variety of seeds
- Dry tempera paint
- Cotton swabs
- Small paper cups
- White glue
- Drawing paper

## Let's Get Involved

1. Bring an hourglass or egg timer to your circle-time gathering. Hold it up, and ask the children to suggest what will happen if you tip it over. Most will say it will spill or pour. Demonstrate how the sand flows back and forth from the top to the bottom.

2. Explain that sand is something that flows easily if it has a space or hole to move through. But, if something gets in the way, the sand is blocked and will not move. Demonstrate this by pouring sand into a paper or Styrofoam cup. Will it pour out of the bottom? Now poke a small hole in the bottom of the cup, and let the children watch to see how it pours out now.

3. Invite the children to stand up and pretend to be some sand in an hourglass. Encourage them to tip one way and then the other as they pretend to flow back and forth. They can experiment with what it feels like to flow and to get blocked.

4. Sing the following song to the tune of "I'm a Little Teapot":

    *I'm an hourglass, filled with sand*
    *Tip me up and watch me flow.*
    *If something blocks me, I cannot go.*
    *Just tip me over, and watch me flow.*

5. Ask the children to think about how it feels when their bodies flow like sand and how it feels when the sand is blocked. Some children may like one feeling more than another. Talk with them about how the sand feels. Have them try making their bodies rigid and hard. Then, have them feel soft and flowing. This is a good way to physically experiencing the difference. Explain that this week they are going to be experimenting with sand and the ways it changes and moves.

## Let's Explore Together

This is an extensive unit of projects, moving from science explorations to movement and art, which you can expand over time.

1. Start the explorations with containers of dry sand. The children will see the experience as different from their regular sandbox play. Continue the conversation about flow. Remind the children of the ideas you shared in circle time.

2. Using the materials you have provided, work together as a group to make predictions. Show the different items, and ask them to guess which ones the sand will flow through and which ones it will not flow through. Sort the items in two piles: *flow* and *no flow.*

3. Give them time to test their hypotheses. Let them take turns using an implement and seeing how the sand flows through it.

4. Allow the children plenty of time to experiment with pouring sand into and out of each of the containers.

5. Ask the children to share their findings with you. Which containers does the sand pour out of? Which containers do not let the sand flow? How can they change a container so that the sand will flow? Yes, add a hole!

6. Help the children add a hole to a plate or cup and watch the results. The children can explore speed by noticing that the sand moves faster when there are more or bigger holes.

7. Feel it with our bodies. Ask the children to pretend that they are in a big box of sand. Encourage them to pretend to put a small hole in the bottom of the sand box and start to slowly flow out. Add bigger and more holes in their "box" so that they are now flowing faster and smoother. End with all the "sand" on the floor in a big pile!

8. Another day, change a variable of your experiment by adding water to the sand. Ask the children to predict what will happen to the flowing sand if they add water to it. Provide a small amount of water for the children to add to the sand. Encourage them to explore the differences between wet and dry sand. Watch them explore all the different ways the sand changes and moves. They may notice that wet sand does not flow through the sieves anymore or that it gets stuck in the colander. They may also notice that it changes color and texture. If possible, write the children's observations on chart paper.

9. If available, bring out your pan balance. Let the children weigh and compare the differences between wet and dry sand. They can put wet on one side and dry on the other. What happens?

10. Let's move again! Ask, "How would your body move if you were dry sand?" Let them move as dry sand. Then, pretend to sprinkle water on the children, and ask them to move again. Ask, "How does your body feel if it is wet sand? How does wet sand move differently from dry?"

## Learning Extensions and Building Community

1. Did you ever wonder if anything grows in sand? Explore growth in sand by having the children plant a variety of seeds in sand-filled egg cartons. Try large seeds as well as small. Water some of them, and leave the others dry. What happens?

2. Bring sand to your art area by mixing sand and dry tempera or grated chalk for the children to explore. Children can use cotton swabs dipped in white glue to draw designs on paper and then sprinkle the sand-paint mixture on top. Shake off the rest, and they have sand paintings!

# Exploring Seeds and Plants

Seeds and plants are classic science activities for young children. Let's put a new twist on these activities by relating the children's own growth and change to the process of growing seeds and plants.

## Science Skills:

- Observing
- Comparing
- Experimenting
- Planting

## Social-Emotional Skills:

- Taking turns
- Listening actively
- Cooperative thinking
- Working together

## Materials:

- A variety of fruits and vegetables that contain seeds, such as snap peas, peppers, tomatoes, apples, oranges, and watermelon
- Plastic knives and forks
- Dried lima beans
- Paper towels
- Unbreakable magnifying glasses
- Paper or plastic cups
- Water
- Potting soil
- Fast-growing seeds, such as nasturtium, peas, squash, watermelon, and zinnia
- Flower boxes
- Mung beans
- Camera (optional)

## Ahead of Time:

Cut the fruits and vegetables in half or quarters for easy exploration.

## Let's Get Involved

1. Start the discussion in your circle time with a song and a game. Welcome the children with a song to the tune of "I'm a Little Teapot."

   *I'm a little "seedie" in the ground*
   *Feeling the rain and hot sun come down.*
   *When I swell and pop [pause] open I'm done!*
   *Sprouting seeds is lots of fun!*

2. Sing it again. This time invite the children to pretend to be a seed in the ground. Pantomime watering and warming them. On the third line, have them pretend to swell and pop open and begin to grow. Ask them, "How big is your plant? Can you make it grow really big? Use your whole body to grow into a giant plant. It is growing just like you are!"

3. Encourage the children to join their "plant" with another "plant" to make a child's garden! Sing the song again as they grow and change together. Ask, "What grows in this garden?"

4. Invite the children to brainstorm their thoughts on growing. They can begin by talking about the experience of growing like a seed. Ask, "Have you grown? Do you grow as fast as a seed? Which are you more like, a plant or a tree? Why?" Help the children listen to each other by modeling active listening. After a child has shared an idea, ask someone to repeat what he heard.

5. End your gathering playing a game similar to the traditional Duck, Duck, Goose. Say, "Seed, seed, sprout; seed, seed, sprout." Eventually add *plant*. On *plant*, the chase begins around the circle!

## Let's Explore Together

1. Create a science lab where the children can explore the growth and change of seeds and plants. Start by looking at where seeds come from. Put out a variety of fruits and vegetables for children to explore. Provide safe plastic knives and forks for opening the halved and quartered fruits and vegetables.

2. Ask the children to find an "investigation partner" to go on a seed hunt together. Invite pairs of children to explore one fruit or vegetable at a time. Ask, "What did you find inside? Where were the seeds? What do they look like?" The teams can sort and classify their seed finds in groups by size, color, or shape.

3. Have the children save the seeds to dry and plant another day. If any fruit or vegetable pieces are still edible, let the children eat them!

4. Provide potting soil and paper cups for planting the seeds they found. Some of the seeds will grow and some will not. However, it is fun to see a grapefruit seed grow in a paper cup!

5. Show the children the dried lima beans. Invite them to try to open one to see inside. Ask them to place the beans in a cup of water overnight to soak. Ask, "What do you think will happen to the seeds after they are in water for a while?" Do not correct them or tell the answer. Explain that they will have a chance to find out tomorrow.

6. Using the lima bean seeds that have soaked overnight, ask the children to find the baby plants inside the seeds. Give each child a paper towel and a few soaked lima beans. Ask them to think about what is inside the bean. Show them how to pull the lima bean apart carefully and see the tiny plant inside. It is helpful to have the children take turns using an unbreakable magnifier to see this. They may like to plant some of the lima beans, too. This will allow them to see how the baby plant becomes a bigger plant, growing just like they do!

7. Grow seeds and sprouts you can eat! This is a good activity to do on a Monday and culminate on a Friday. Show the children how to grow edible sprouts such as mung beans. Place the mung beans between layers of wet paper towels. These will grow to edible size by the end of the week. Have the children create a graph of the growth process by taking one bean out each day and gluing it on a strip of cardboard. Ask, "How does the mung bean look different each day? How has it changed? How has it grown?" Make a salad with mung bean sprouts on Friday or put them on a peanut butter sandwich. Delicious!

8.  The children can work cooperatively to create a class garden indoors that can be taken outside. Use fast-growing seeds that provide quick results, such as nasturtium and zinnia, as well as beans and squashes. Start the seeds in potting soil inside by a sunny window. Eventually take them outside to the playground. The children can work together to observe the growth of the seeds and plants each day. Use a camera to take photos of the growth, or have the children make drawings each day in a science journal. Inspire the children to work together to predict when they think their seeds will appear. They can mark the date on the calendar with their initials.

## Learning Extensions and Building Community

1.  Use seedlings to experiment with a plant's need for light and water. Invite the children to make predictions about what the seedlings need. What is the best place to grow our seedlings? Is more water or light always best? Test and see!
2.  Read stories about seeds and plants, such as *The Little Red Hen* by Paul Galdone, *The Carrot Seed* by Ruth Krauss, and *Growing Vegetable Soup* by Lois Ehlert. Each book provides an opportunity for the children to reflect on the cooperative nature of gardening and the process of growing.
3.  Send the children home with some fast-growing seeds to plant with their families. The children can plant them in an egg carton or outside in the yard.
4.  Adopt a plant in the playground. Observation of growth is an important science skill. Children may like to find a small flower or even a weed to observe over the course of the spring and summer. At first, they will probably be bigger than the plant. But some plants may grow bigger than they are. Ask, "Do you grow as fast as this plant?"
5.  Some cultures use seeds for art. Children may like to make seed collages or mosaics using a wide variety of seeds from the store or from the fruits and vegetables you have been using. They can glue the seeds to a small paper plate or press them into clay or playdough.
6.  People eat seeds such as sunflower and popcorn. Serve some sunflower seeds or make popcorn for a snack.

**SEL SPOTLIGHT**
Cooperative planting activities invite children to work together to explore a new concept and the scientific process. Young children are building the same problem-solving and cooperative-thinking skills that they will need to work with lab partners in high school.

# Getting to the Heart of Language

## CHAPTER 4

Language is an essential element of social and emotional growth. It is through their communication of thoughts and feelings that children learn to express themselves. These language activities are designed to encourage children to verbally share within the whole group as well as in smaller group activities. They will build vocabulary and the ability to speak in front of a group. Through language activities, children will learn appropriate language for feelings and social communication. The art of speaking and listening is a joy that children will develop not only in the early years but also throughout their schooling. Let's play with language together.

# I Like the Way!

When you give real compliments, you create a setting that is positive and welcoming to children. Plus, you inspire children to add these words and phrases to their daily vocabulary. Young children love to get compliments, but they are just learning how to give them.

**Materials:**

- Chart paper or whiteboard
- Drawing paper
- Old magazines
- Glue sticks
- Safety scissors
- Assorted collage materials, such as feathers, fabric, and ribbon
- Crayons and markers
- Small tree branch

**Language Skills:**

- Expressive vocabulary
- Noticing
- Listening
- Sharing

**Social-Emotional Skills:**

- Giving compliments
- Feeling acceptance
- Listening to others
- Expressing caring and concern

## Let's Get Involved

1. You can use a compliment song to welcome the children to circle time in a positive way. As you sing, you are reinforcing the children's positive behavior and are modeling complimenting. You can sing about whatever you want to reinforce and celebrate—sitting, listening, waiting—any gerund that fits. Sing to the tune of "Here We Go 'Round the Mulberry Bush."

   *I like the way that Susi is sitting,*
   *John is sitting, and George is sitting.*
   *I like the way that everyone's sitting,*
   *So now it's time for circle.*

2. Talk about the song. Ask, "How did you feel when I sang your name?" Ask what you said about each child. Explain that when you like something that someone does, you can give a compliment: "I like the way" and then say what you like. Compliments feel good! It feels good to hear that someone likes what you did or said, and it feels best when she tells you what she liked.

3. Remind the children that sometimes you compliment them on something they are wearing to school: "I sang that I liked the way you were sitting, but I could sing that I like your red shirt today." Sing the following lyrics

to the tune of "Way Down Yonder in the Pawpaw Patch" to call out the different colors and clothing the children are wearing. Add a fun word at the end of the song to illustrate more compliment words.

*Who is, who is, who's wearing red?*
*Who is, who is, who's wearing red?*
*Who is, who is, who's wearing red?*
*Stand up and take a bow! Beautiful!*

4. Continue the game with different *colors* or *pieces* of clothing. Be sure that every child gets to stand for the song and to hear a compliment.

## Let's Explore Together

1. Start a compliment board in your literacy area. Ask the children to suggest words and phrases to say when they want to compliment someone. You may have to model and start with simple words such as *great, super, cool, excellent,* or *amazing.* Write the words on chart paper or the whiteboard. Add a small image or decoration for each word to help the children recognize it. Over time, you can add more words and phrases. As you review the board with the children, ask, "How does it feel when someone tells you that you are super or great?"

2. Make compliment cards for sharing. The children may want to copy the words from the compliment board to make their cards. You can choose a word a day to focus on in the literacy area. Provide materials for the children to draw or copy the word and add illustrations. Ask, "Who will you give a compliment to today?"

3. Do not forget *thank you!* Often children get carried away with making compliment cards. It is so much fun to play with these words and give them away. Extend the learning by talking about the importance of saying thank you when someone compliments you. Show the children how to write thank-you cards, too. Pretty soon, you will have a lot of card giving going back and forth!

4. Compliments make people smile! Provide drawing paper, old magazines, and art materials for the children to use to create smile pictures. They can find smiling faces, cut them out, and paste them on their collages. Talk to the children about the images: "Why do you think this person is smiling? What do you think someone said to make him smile? What could you say?"

## Learning Extensions and Building Community

1. Make a compliment tree. The children can "write" and decorate compliment words on cards and attach them to a branch in the classroom. Then, when they want to give a compliment to someone, they can pick it off the tree and give it away. You never know what you will get!

2. High five! Create a compliment movement or ritual with the group. Most children are familiar with a high five, but challenge them to think of another movement to do to show appreciation. Let them share their ideas, then choose a movement to use. Use it for a period of time, and reinforce it throughout the day. Way to go!

3. Play a compliment version of Duck, Duck, Goose outside on the playground. Seat the children in a circle in a large open area. Let the leader walk around the circle lightly tapping heads then stop at a child and offer a compliment. The other child says thank you and then takes a turn.

4. Send the children home with compliment cards. Families will love to use them, too!

**SEL SPOTLIGHT**

Modeling is one of the best ways to teach children the words for compliments. Exaggerate each time you offer a specific compliment word. Say it, repeat it, smile, and say it again.

# Friendship Circle

Young children need activities that help them feel comfortable and accepted in the group. This grounding is essential for cognitive as well as social development. The early relationships forged in your classroom become the model for the future.

**Language Skills:**

- Expressive vocabulary
- Speaking in a group
- Sharing an idea

**Social-Emotional Skills:**

- Making friends
- Seeking peers as play partners
- Feeling accepted in the group
- Asking permission

**Materials:**

- Mural paper
- Crayons and markers
- Drawing paper
- Timer
- Fingerpaint
- Fingerpaint paper
- Children's books on friendship (optional)

## Let's Get Involved

1. Something special happens when you gather children together in a circle. Perhaps it is because a circle has no beginning or end, or perhaps it is because everyone is seen equally. Within the circle, children feel safe to share, express feelings, and learn from each other. Use a rhyme to welcome the children in a positive way, to the rhythm of

   "'Round and 'Round the Garden":
   *Round and 'round the circle,*
   *Look at who is here.*
   *One friend, two friends,*
   *I see you all so clear!*

2. Celebrate the circle of friends by repeating the rhyme, pointing to a pair of children as you chant. Each time, at the end, have the two children welcome each other in a fun way. They can wave, shake, wiggle their noses, or wink! Repeat as many times as needed for each pair to feel welcome.

3. Write the question, "What is a friend?" on chart paper, and invite the children to brainstorm many ideas of what a friend is and does. Write down their ideas. This activity can be revisited many times at circle time. Each time you do it, you will be expanding children's friendship vocabulary.

4. Turn the children's words describing a friend into a class poem. On each line, write, "A friend is," and finish the sentence with one of the children's words.

*A friend is kind.*
*A friend is helpful.*
*A friend is fun.*
*A friend is playful.*

## Let's Explore Together

1. Consider making a friends center in your room. Stock it with books, paper, markers and crayons, and anything else that you can think of to support learning about friendship. There, the children can explore language, art, and community. This area will invite the children to discover many ways of expressing friendship.

2. How are we all connected? By our friendship paths! Place a sheet of mural paper on the floor or on a large table. Seat the children around the outside edge of the paper.

3. Give them markers and crayons, and encourage them to draw a self-portrait on the part of the paper that is in front of them.

4. Ask them to draw a path from themselves to their friends' self portraits. Make sure that every child is connected to at least one other child.

5. Look at the friendship map. Where do the paths intersect? What does the map design look like? The children may like to name their roads and streets.

6. Display the map of friends on a bulletin board in the friends center.

7. Sharing can be hard for some children, particularly when it comes to their artwork, but you can make it into a game. Seat the children around a table. Provide drawing paper and crayons for free drawing. Explain that you are going to turn on a timer. When it rings, they are to pass their picture to a friend who will add something to the picture.

8. Let them start drawing. Set the timer for three minutes. When it rings, ask them to pass their own drawings to a friend and then draw on a friend's picture.

9. Continue all the way around the table until each picture is back to its original owner.

10. Encourage the children to talk about the activity and their pictures. What did their friends draw?

11. There is something so wonderful about making a mess with a friend. Provide all the materials needed for free exploration of fingerpainting on mural or fingerpaint paper.

12. At the end of the activity, have the children make a friendship wreath for the classroom door. Draw a big circle on a piece of drawing paper, and let the children place one handprint along the edge. A circle of friends!

## Learning Extensions and Building Community

1. Bring friendship to two-sided easels as an extension of the pass-along pictures. Let each child paint a few strokes on paper on her side of the easel and, when a bell rings, switch to the other side. The children can go back and forth to create two cooperative pictures!

2. Take the friendship games outside with a version of Mother May I. Let one child be the leader, and ask the others to stand several feet away in a line in front of him.

3. The children ask, "Friend, may I take one big step?" and the leader answers, "Yes, you may," or "No, you can't." The goal is to get to the other side of the space. Continue as long as the children are interested, letting several children be the leader in turn.

4. Have the children form two concentric circles, one inside the other. Play music and encourage the circles to move in opposite directions.

5. When the music stops, ask the children to stop and turn to face someone in the opposite circle. Encourage them to shake hands, spin each other around, or give a high five!

6. Start and stop the music several times so the children can acknowledge different friends.

**SEL SPOTLIGHT**

In the early days of early childhood education, the main focus was on helping children learn how to make friends. While there are a great deal more academic pressures on children now, we can keep that focus in everything we do. Friends games and activities should happen throughout the year, not just at the beginning. Like an ever-revolving spiral, each time a child revisits an activity, she meets it at a new level of competence.

# The Sound and Rhythm of Words

Young children are just beginning to explore the sounds, rhythms, and feel of words.

**Language Skills:**

- Listening
- Expressive vocabulary
- Rhythm
- Rhyming

**Social-Emotional Skills:**

- Listening
- Following directions
- Developing self-awareness
- Seeing self as a member in a group

**Materials:**

- Sturdy paper plates
- Markers and crayons
- Dried beans or seeds, bells, or sand
- Stapler
- Collage and nature materials (optional)

## Let's Get Involved

Have you ever noticed that the best way to get children's attention is to sing to them? Young children often will stop everything when they hear music. Much like the Pied Piper, you can use music to lead your students to learning.

1. Start with a simple sound and rhythm call-and-response game. In a singsong voice say, "Hello." Repeat it several times with the same sound and inflection. Invite the children to try it, too: "Can you say hello just like I did? I will say it, and you say it back to me. Hello!"

2. Expand the game by adding clapping. Clap the two beats of the word as you say it again. See if children can do it, too.

3. Add another word to the call and response: "Hello, friends." Call the words again, and invite the children to respond. Add clapping, too!

4. Try it with the children's names. Call out a child's name and ask the child to echo it. Add claps to go with the name, too. Invite all the children to say and clap the friend's name. Children will enjoy hearing the group say their names in a special rhythmic way.

5. Invite the children to tap and say their own name while others are saying theirs. It might sound like a swamp at night, but it will be fun!

6. Show the children your handmade tambourine, demonstrating how you can tap it to a rhythm. Tell the children they are going to be making their own tambourines this week!

**Ahead of Time:**

- Make a paper-plate tambourine for demonstration: Lay one paper plate facedown on top of another plate that is faceup. Staple the edges, leaving a gap. Put dried beans, sand, or bells into the pocket you have created, then staple the gap closed. Decorate the tambourine any way you wish.

- Before the Let's Explore Together activity, set out the materials for the tambourines in the art center.

## Let's Explore Together

1. Invite the children to the art table with a rhythmic greeting, saying and beating the word *welcome* on your tambourine. Invite the children to say and clap it with you. You can reinforce the name game from circle time by asking the children to say and clap their names in greeting.

2. Show the children how to put the plates together, fronts facing each other. Help them carefully staple the edges to make a pocket. Remember to leave a gap.

3. Let them fill their tambourines with small items such as dried beans or bells. Staple the gaps closed.

4. The surface of the tambourine is an inviting blank canvas waiting to be decorated. Provide a wide variety of art materials from crayons and markers to collage or nature materials for the children to use to decorate their tambourines.

5. Once the children have created their very own tambourines, they will want to use them. There should be a whole lot of shakin' going on in the room. Organize it all into a tambourine song that the children can easily learn to sing and play. Sing to the tune of "Here We Go 'Round the Mulberry Bush."

   *The tambourines have come to town,*
   *Come to town,*
   *Come to town.*
   *The tambourines have come to town*
   *To play for all their friends.*

6. Explore the sounds of the children's names with the tambourines. Shake the tambourines to the beat of each child's name.

7. One of the interesting things children learn from this exploration is that music and sound can express emotions. Invite the children to play their tambourines as you all sing a round of the classic, "If You're Happy And You Know It."

8. Ask the children to experiment with making different types of sounds with their tambourines. Can they make a shy sound, an angry sound, a scary sound, a quiet sound, and a sleepy sound? Sing the song again, changing the emotion each time.

9. Use the tambourines to play a simple three-part pattern, such as tap, tap, rattle; tap, tap, rattle. Invite the children to repeat the pattern. Add

words to the beat, or let the children count it out as you play. After the children have learned the pattern, try a new one. Eventually, invite them to make up their own patterns for a Follow the Leader game.

## Learning Extensions and Building Community

.   Ask the children to bring their tambourines to circle time. Read a familiar rhyme, such as "One, Two, Buckle My Shoe," and ask the children to shake the rhythm with you.

2.   Play with rhythm and rhyme with circle dancing games. There are several classics that will work with tambourines, such as "Ring around the Rosie"; "Go In and Out the Windows"; and of course, "The Hokey Pokey."

3.   Challenge the children to say a familiar rhyme while they are clapping and walking around the circle—not easy to do!

**SEL SPOTLIGHT**
**Many young children have a difficult time listening in a group. There are so many distractions, and sometimes there are just too many words to listen to! Listening and speaking games hone these skills with light, fun, and deep meaning. Play listening games every day!**

# So Big!

Children are fascinated with size. They want to be big and are becoming very aware of the sizes of everything in their world. This is a great time to learn words for comparative size.

## Language Skills:

- Size words
- Comparative language
- Sequencing
- Storytelling

## Social-Emotional Skills:

- Sharing ideas in the group
- Expressing collective creativity
- Listening

## Materials:

- Objects in a variety of sizes, such as toys, dolls, books, or cars
- Toys for storytelling in a range of sizes from very small to large
- Box or pillowcase
- Drawing paper
- Glue sticks
- Markers and crayons
- Chart paper or whiteboard
- Nesting matryoshka dolls (optional)
- Toy balls in three sizes
- Felt story board with "Goldilocks and the Three Bears" characters (optional)

## Ahead of Time:

- Put a collection of objects of different sizes in a box or bag. Try to find similar objects of various sizes, such as a sequence of toys, books, cars, or dolls. The nesting matryoshka dolls are wonderful for this.
- Draw three circles on a piece of paper: big, bigger, and biggest. Make copies to use in the literacy area.

## Let's Get Involved

1. Start your circle time with a chant about size words.

   *I've got a little clap—it goes like this.* (clap softly)
   *I've got a bigger clap—it goes like this.* (clap a little harder)
   *I've got more claps—they go like this.* (clap loudly)
   *Big, bigger, biggest!* (clap, clap, clap)
   *Little, littler, littlest!* (clap, clap, clap)

   After you have offered the chant one time, invite the children to clap along with you.

2. Talk about the size words you just used. Invite the children to think about the gradations of size by showing the words with their hands. "Can you show me big?" "Can you show me bigger?" "Can you show me biggest?"

3. Write the words on chart paper or the whiteboard. Help the children notice that not only does the sound of the words get bigger but each succeeding word is also bigger than the one before it. Count how many letters are in each word. Which has the most?

4. Play a short movement game to keep the children involved with the topic and each other. Invite the children to stand up and find a partner. Ask the pairs to do a big movement together. They can move their hands, legs, or whole bodies.

5.   Challenge the pairs to make the movement bigger. How do they move now?

6.   Ask them to make the biggest movement they can together!

7.   If there is time and interest, have children do it again with *little, littler, littlest.*

## Let's Explore Together

Move the activity to your literacy center where you can offer the activities in small groups. This will allow the children more opportunity to work with the materials.

1.   Gather a small group at a table for a size story. Show your story bag (or box), and explain that you are going to tell a story using the things inside.

2.   Ask a child to reach inside the bag and pull out an object. Use it to start the story—for example, "Once upon a time there was a **small** cat. It was having a lovely day but then . . ."

3.   Pass the bag to the next child, and ask him to take out the next object for you to use to continue the story. Emphasize size words as you tell the story: "along came a **smaller** bird that flew over the **small** cat." Place the objects on the table as they are used so that the children can see the differences in the sizes.

4.   Continue the story until all the objects are on the table. Invite the children to notice the big and little things as well as the biggest and littlest.

5.   Encourage the children to order the objects in rows from smallest to largest.

6.   Now it is their turn to be creative together. Put all the items back into the container, and invite the children to tell their own story with your help. It works best if you start the story. Then, have the children take turns pulling out an object and adding to the story. This is a "let's do it again" activity that children will want to do repeatedly. Periodically, add some new items to the collection to expand the story and the exploration of size words.

7.   Provide paper and art materials for the children to draw the story.

8.   Give the children drawing paper with images of three different circles: big, bigger, biggest. Invite the children to draw or paste images in the circles to show the sizes.

9. Write a size word on a chart in the literacy area. Have the children suggest the *littlest* or *biggest* things they know. Make a list of their ideas!

## Learning Extensions and Building Community

1. Record the stories the children tell. Children love to hear their own voices. Place the recording in your literacy area. Children will love to hear it over and over again and can use the objects to act out the story as they are listening to it.

2. Use a familiar story such as "The Three Bears." Children can work with the words for size as Goldilocks makes her way through the house! Invite the children to use their hands to show Papa-, Mama-, and Baby-sized items. You can also use a felt board to tell the story and to show the three different sizes.

3. Play a group circle game with size words. Let the children roll big, bigger, and biggest balls across the circle when they hear the appropriate word: "Roll the **bigger** ball, not the **big** one and not the **biggest**."

**SEL SPOTLIGHT**

Children can sometimes be afraid of making mistakes and will not offer any ideas in a group setting. As young children mature, they begin to feel more comfortable sharing their ideas. It is helpful for children to know that there is no right or wrong way to tell a story. Support the children in saying their ideas without fear of criticism.

# Will I Have a Friend?

Children sometimes wonder if they will have a friend when they go off to school. Just one friend can make a world of difference for a child's sense of place in the group. Explore all the ways we can make a new toy feel comfortable in our class, and build a vocabulary of caring, empathy, and friendship.

## Materials:

- New doll or stuffed toy
- Large box or pillowcase
- Name cards
- Timer
- Drawing paper
- Markers and crayons
- Chart paper or whiteboard

## Language Skills:

- Expressive language
- Emotion vocabulary
- Storytelling

## Social-Emotional Skills:

- Feeling empathy for others
- Caring for others
- Helping
- Suggesting play themes and activities to peers

## Ahead of Time:

Hide the new doll or stuffed toy in the pillowcase or box.

## Let's Get Involved

At this stage of development, children may be too shy to express their feelings and empathy for others. Interestingly, a toy can be the perfect tool for this because children can communicate with it in very simple ways. Plus, it does not talk back—usually!

1.  Welcome the children to circle with your favorite welcoming song, or introduce a new one. Changes to circle time expand children's thinking and experience. Try this song, sung to the tune of "Mary Had a Little Lamb":

    *Welcome to our class today, class today, class today.*
    *Welcome to our class today.*
    *We are glad you're here.*

2.  Help the children feel welcomed as a friend by singing a verse with their name in it.

    *Welcome to our friend today, friend today, friend today.*
    *Welcome to our friend today.*
    *Rachel is here!*

3. Show the children your surprise package. Invite them to guess what might be inside. If it is in a pillowcase, you can pass the package around for the children to feel and guess.

4. Be dramatic! Peek inside the bag, and give the children a clue. "Well, I have a new friend for our classroom hiding inside. But, he is kind of shy and is not sure if he wants to join us. Did you ever feel shy about coming to school? Well, he feels that way, too. Let's sing the song again to welcome him, and maybe he will join us!"

5. Sing the song together, perhaps several times, and eventually have the toy peek out and look around. The children are bound to be excited and will want to touch. Remind them how it feels to be new to a group. "We need to be quiet and gentle so he does not get frightened, okay?"

6. Take the toy around the circle, and invite each child to touch it with a soft pat and say, "Welcome."

7. When you return to your place, set the toy on your lap as you continue the conversation. Tell the children that the toy is feeling a bit more comfortable. Thank them for welcoming him with such caring. Reinforce the word *care* as you talk about the experience.

8. Ask the children to share how they felt when they first came to the class. "How did you feel when you first walked through the door? How did you feel in circle time? What helped you feel happy to be here?" Listen to their responses.

9. Enlist the children's help. Ask them to suggest what they can do to help the new toy feel comfortable in class today. Suggest that small groups take turns showing the toy around the learning centers of the room.

## Let's Explore Together

1. The children will all want to play with the new toy right away, so create an organized way to show the toy around the classroom. Tell the children that you will divide them into small groups, and each group can show the toy one learning center. Choose three or four name cards, and tell the children that that group will be the first hosts. They can choose a center to show their new friend. Talk about what they will do with the toy as they show it around. What would it want to know about the dramatic play area or the blocks? How can they make the toy feel comfortable in the new area?

2. Turn on a timer, and send the first group off on their hosting task. When the bell rings, the first group can return to the table and tell you what

they did together. Provide paper and art supplies for the children to draw pictures of their new friend and what they did. Be available to take their dictation of the experience.

3. Send the next group out to a new center while this group is drawing. Continue in this manner, and make sure that all of the children have a chance to welcome the toy and show it around.

4. Collect the pictures and stories into a class book: *Tales of our New Friend.*

5. Another day, the children may like to brainstorm a list of names for the new friend in your literacy center. Make a list of the names on chart paper or the whiteboard. Children can vote for their favorite with a tally mark on the list.

## Learning Extensions and Building Community

1. Ask the children to help you create a list of caring words in the literacy center. Focus on one word at a time. Choose words such as *kind, care, quiet, help,* and *listen.* Post the words for all to see.

2. Revisit the progress of the new friend's activities in a group meeting. At the end of the day, ask the children to share what they did to help the new friend feel comfortable.

3. Invite families to participate in the friendship building. After several weeks, set up a schedule to send the new toy home for a weekend visit. On Monday, the child can share what they did together!

**SEL SPOTLIGHT**
**Hands-on caring activities help children develop a caring vocabulary they can use with each other and themselves. The more concrete and practical you make the experiences, the more applicable the understanding.**

# The Three Ws

We all want young children to love books. Books provide so many wonderful opportunities for exploring language and character and for building a love of stories and words. Let's explore the who, what, and where of books together!

**Materials:**

- A collection of your favorite picture books
- Drawing paper
- Markers and crayons
- Chart paper or whiteboard

**Language Skills:**

- Book vocabulary
- Investigative language
- Critical thinking
- Storytelling

**Social-Emotional Skills:**

- Collective brainstorming
- Decision making
- Expressing creatively

**Ahead of Time:**

Make a "Who, What, Where" chart. Write the words at the top of the page, leaving room for the children to add their ideas in the columns below.

## Let's Get Involved

Studies of the who, what, and where of books open the door to book talk that can span your entire year of reading together. To keep things simple, you may want to do just one or two Ws per session.

1. Start circle time with a book! Choose a class favorite that everyone knows. Tell the children, "I was looking at all of our wonderful books, and I remembered this one that we like very much. I am going to read it again. Can anyone remember anything about the story?" Encourage the children to share what they remember.

2. Read the story, inviting the children to join in on any parts they can help with.

3. Direct the children's attention to the "Who, What, Where" chart. Help them notice that all the words start with the same letter: *W.* Read the chart. Explain that they are going to use the chart to be book investigators. Every story has a who, what, and where.

4. Inspire collective brainstorming with a song sung to the tune of "Row, Row, Row Your Boat."

   *Who, who, who is it*
   *In our storybook?*
   *Who, who, who is it?*
   *Let's all take a look.*

5. Encourage the children to look at the book you have chosen and share who the characters are. You can point to the cover and the pages of the book to help the children focus their thinking. Write their answers under *who* on the chart.

6. Now, a bit more challenging question is, "What happens in the story?" Ask them to think about what the character does. Write the children's ideas on the appropriate part of the chart. The children may not always agree on this one. This is good because it creates more opportunities for discussion and decision making.

7. Ask the children to think about where the story takes place. This can be a bit more challenging for children because they often are more interested in the who and what of the story. Go back to the book and ask the children to use the illustrations to help the conversation. Add their ideas to the chart. Now they are book investigators and have discovered the who, what, and where of a book!

## Let's Explore Together

1. Carry the investigations into your literacy area where the children can explore all of their favorite books. Bring a collection of favorite books to the table, and invite the children to explore the covers.

2. Ask them to sort the books in many different ways; for example, they can sort by who is in the story: animal characters or people characters. Or, they can sort by where the story takes place: city, country, inside, outside, and so on.

3. Talk about favorite characters. Who do they like best? Why? Provide art materials for the children to create drawings of their favorite characters. Display these in the literacy area with the children's dictation.

4. Work together to create a Favorite Character Graph. The children can name their favorite characters, and then the class can vote on the graph for their choice. Look at the graph together, and help the children decide who won the vote.

5. Invite the children to explore their favorite settings in books. Ask, "Where does your favorite story happen? Is it outside or inside? Is it warm or cold?" Provide art materials for the children to use as they draw or paint the settings of their favorite story.

6. Some stories and settings can be upsetting for children because at this stage of development they are not always sure if the story is real or pretend. Invite the children to explore your collection of favorite books

and sort the books into two categories: real and pretend. Ask, "How do you know when something is real or pretend?" Help the children begin to tell the difference. There may be some discussion on this one, because some children want a character to be real!

## Learning Extensions and Building Community

1.  I'm Thinking of a Book is a great guessing game that invites children to explore what they know about books and characters. Give the children clues to a familiar story or book and let them try to guess it! "I'm thinking of a character who goes to visit some bears and eats their food. What story is it?"
2.  Use a new book to extend the learning. Show the book, focusing on the cover. Invite the children to use clues in the illustration to predict who the story is about, where it might take place, and even suggest what will happen. Then, read the book to find out!
3.  Collect the children's favorite books together to set up a favorite-book lending library. Share the children's choices with families at the end of this exploration. The children can share what they have learned as book investigators!

**SEL SPOTLIGHT**
Group brainstorming is important for children's social development. Throughout their school years, they will be asked to share their ideas with a group, to listen to each other, and to collectively come to agreements. Your practical large- and small-group activities lay the foundation for this important skill.

# Crazy Questions!

Children love to ask why. In this fun activity, you turn the tables and ask them!

## Materials:

- Plastic circle bracelet
- Interesting items, such as a tool, a piece of jewelry, and a kitchen utensil
- Picture of a thunderstorm or rainbow
- Drawing paper
- Watercolors
- Markers and crayons
- Fabric bag
- Variety of paper shapes
- Glue

## Language Skills:

- Creative thinking
- Brainstorming
- Storytelling

## Social-Emotional Skills:

- Sharing ideas with a group
- Decision making
- Expressing creatively
- Helping

## Let's Get Involved

Introduce the concept of open-ended, crazy questions in your group, but be prepared for the children to be cautious at first and copy each other's answers. Over time, the children will become more comfortable sharing an idea that is their very own.

1. Start the fun by playing dumb or forgetful. The children will love to help you, and you will get the conversation going with a great deal of interest. Show the plastic bracelet or anything else you want to use. Explain that you were getting ready for school and you forgot what this was. Ask the children to help you. "What is it? What am I supposed to do with it?" Be silly and demonstrate some crazy ideas to keep the conversation going. "Do I put it on my head? Do I use it to drive the car? What else could I do with it?"

2. Expand the thinking and problem solving by asking the children to think of all the different things the object could be or how to use it. If they get stuck, offer a fun idea, such as, "It could be a hula-hoop for a squirrel!"

3. Compliment the children on their creative thinking together. Celebrate their answers equally and with joy. Remind them that there is no wrong answer, so they can suggest whatever they like. Tell them, "This is called *brainstorming*—a funny word but it is kind of like the ideas are storming in your head."

## Ahead of Time:

- Collect some unusual items for exploring with open-ended questions. Look for an interesting tool, piece of jewelry, or a kitchen utensil. An egg separator is a good one!
- On several sheets of paper, glue two shapes per paper, making sure that no two papers are alike.

## Let's Explore Together

1.  It is good to ask open-ended questions in small groups. Children tend to be more open to sharing and will be less likely to copy each other. Crazy questions can start with an object and expand into a concept. They lead beautifully to art and writing. Offer a crazy question. Ask the children if they ever wonder about things. Show a picture of a thunderstorm or rainbow. Ask, "Where do you think thunderstorms come from? What makes a thunderstorm?" Remember, this is about creative thinking, not fact. So, there is no wrong answer, and the more creative the better!

2.  Provide watercolors and paper for the children to use to paint their thunderstorms. As they work, talk with the children one-on-one about their paintings. Ask them to tell you more about where it came from or what made the thunderstorm. Post these comments and pictures on a bulletin board, or put them together in a class book.

3.  Put out a gab bag of interesting and unusual items in your literacy area. Periodically, have the children reach inside and choose something to gab about. Talk about what the object could be and how it could be used. Be silly and creative! This also works well as a simple circle or transition activity.

4.  Bring crazy questions to your easel. Take away the brushes, and add something unusual to paint with, such as a feather, a corncob, or a spoon. Challenge the children to try painting with the new item.

5.  Extend into an art and language activity. Bring out the papers with shapes glued to them that you created ahead of time. Have the children choose a sheet, and incorporate the shapes into pictures they create on the paper. Perhaps a circle becomes a ball or a triangle a roof. Invite the children to tell you about their art!

## Learning Extensions and Building Community

1.  Children love helping, especially when you pretend to have forgotten something. When you let them help, you reinforce their creative thinking. At circle time, show the children the materials for the day's art project, and tell them you forgot what they were going to do with it. Ask for their ideas.

2. Add crazy questions to story time. Read a book together, and then ask the children to suggest a new ending for the story or to change one of the characters. "What if Clifford were a cat? How would the story be different?"

3. Invite the families to play with language, too. Send home a book with a crazy-question card inside for families to use together. It will make for great dinnertime conversation. You can also send home cards with fun questions that they often hear their children ask, such as, "Why is the sky blue?" or "Why do birds fly?" Encourage them to try to think of creative answers to these questions with their children. And, these questions can be a great way to keep their children entertained in the grocery line.

**SEL SPOTLIGHT**
Often, when we ask children an open-ended question, the first answer is a shrug and "I don't know." They do not want to be wrong in front of the group. When children realize that there is no wrong answer, they slowly become more secure about sharing ideas with the group.

# My Words and Me

Young children need lots of practice with the words for emotions. When they have the vocabulary for the nuances of feeling, they tend to express their emotions with greater ease and clarity.

## Materials:

- Old magazines
- Scissors
- Glue
- Card stock
- Drawing paper
- Markers and crayons
- Chart paper or whiteboard
- Poster board
- Camera
- Balloons
- Funnel
- Cornstarch
- Spoon
- Recorded music
- Mural paper
- Masking tape

## Language Skills:

- Expressive vocabulary
- Creative expression
- Communication

## Social-Emotional Skills:

- Sharing feelings
- Decision making
- Taking turns
- Social interaction

## Ahead of Time:

- Make emotion picture cards for discussion. Cut photos from magazines of faces representing different emotions. Paste these on card stock.
- Make event picture cards. Cut magazine photos of events that express emotions. Look for photos of surprises, problems, celebrations, and so on. Paste these on card stock.

## Let's Get Involved

1. Make the words for emotions visual and kinesthetic for children. The concept of *happy* is abstract until you have an expression or an action to go with it. Let's start with some games to get things going. Play Make a Face to get children excited about working with facial expressions. Tell the children, "I am going to make a face and pass it to the person next to me. That person will make the same funny face and pass it to the next person. We will go all the way around the circle so everyone has a chance to make a funny face."

2. Make a silly smile or funny face, and turn to the child to your right so she can see it. She then makes a face just like yours and turns and passes it to the next child in the circle.

3. Continue the game, adding emotions such as happy, grumpy, shy, and sad. Social-emotional learning takes place as children begin to feel comfortable expressing emotions within the safe confines of the game.

4. Share the emotions cards with the group. Talk about the images. Ask, "How do you think this person is feeling?" Choose words to go with each card.

5. Have the children take turns choosing a card that shows how they feel today. They might be tired, happy, or excited. Talk with them about their choices.

6.  Sing a song to invite the children to talk about feelings. They can use the card to add their feeling to the song, sung to the tune of "Row, Row, Row Your Boat":

    *Friend, friend, friend of mine,* (everyone sings together)
    *How are you today?*
    *I feel (emotion).* (one child says an emotion)
    *We're glad you shared today!* (everyone sings together)

7.  Another day, extend the conversation at circle time by using sentence starters for the children to finish. You could say, "I'm happy when…." Or, say, "I'm sad when…." This simple technique is surprisingly successful for inviting children to discuss their feelings.

## Let's Explore Together

1.  Children love to make faces! Take photos of the children expressing different emotions.
2.  Print out the photos and glue them onto drawing paper, then invite the children to add illustrations.
3.  Put the emotion pictures out in the center for discussion. The children can sort the pictures according to happy or sad emotions or any other way they choose.
4.  Put all of the photo sheets together to create a class book of feelings.
5.  Sometimes an emotion arises out of an event. Introduce the event pictures you created. Choose one of the pictures, and ask the children to talk about what they think is happening in the photo. How are the people feeling? What are they doing? What is happening?
6.  Invite the children to do some imagining about the event. This will provide them with the experience of using context to interpret emotions. The children may like to draw a picture of a happy conclusion to the event.
7.  Music can inspire emotion. Tape a large sheet of mural paper to the floor or table. Provide markers or crayons for the children to use as they listen to music.
8.  As the children draw, play a variety of music. Stop between each selection, and ask the children to think about how each feels. Then, invite them to draw how it feels.
9.  Make simple stress balls. Work one-on-one with children to choose a balloon color that expresses how they are feeling today. Hold a funnel

in the opening of the balloon as the child slowly spoons cornstarch into the ball. Do not fill it too much. Tie it off, and give it a squeeze!

## Learning Extensions and Building Community

1. Storybook characters have emotions, too! Invite the children to think about the emotions of characters during story time. How is the character feeling? Why? What might happen next?

2. Create an emotions check-in circle for the classroom. On a piece of poster board, draw a large circle and cut it out. Place drawings or photos for different feelings on the outside edge of the circle. Make a name clothespin for each child. When they arrive at school they can clip their name on the emotion they are feeling that day.

**SEL SPOTLIGHT**

Sometimes it is just too difficult for children to share their emotions. Many will be willing to watch and listen to an activity but not to share. It is important to give children permission not to share and to go to a quiet place to rest for a while if an activity is just too much for them.

# It's Not Fair!

Young children have a heightened sense of fairness that often is quite literal. It is important for children to participate in practical activities that explore the concept of fairness as they build a vocabulary for speaking fairly and resolving conflict.

### Language Skills:

- Expressive vocabulary
- Creative expression
- Communication

### Social-Emotional Skills:

- Using words to resolve conflict
- Calming behaviors
- Taking turns
- Waiting

### Materials:

- Small objects or counters, two or three less than needed to give every child five
- Fabric or paper bag
- Can or box
- Construction paper
- Tape
- Drawing paper
- Markers and crayons
- Tongue depressors
- Chart paper or whiteboard
- Book that addresses feelings vocabulary, such as *Words Are Not for Hurting* by Elizabeth Verdick

### Ahead of Time:

Cover a can or box with construction paper. Write the words *My Turn* on the outside.

## Let's Get Involved

1. Introduce the activity with a story that you make up! You can tell a story about a time when you felt something was not fair, such as when someone pushed in front of you in line or when someone did not return something he borrowed. Keep it simple and share how the experience felt to you.

2. Ask the children, "Did you ever feel that way? Do you ever feel like something isn't fair?" Ask them to share their experiences with the group. Ask, "How did it feel? What did you do about it?"

3. Read a book about feelings and using kind vocabulary, such as *Words Are Not for Hurting* by Elizabeth Verdick. Talk with the children about using kind words, and teach them kind vocabulary words that they can say to each other.

4. Ask the children to reflect on fairness. Suggest what it means to be fair. Ask, "How are we fair at school? How do we play fair in a game?" Write the children's ideas on chart paper or the whiteboard.

5. Talk with the children about what they can do when something does not feel fair. Brainstorm ideas for how to handle a situation. Write a list of positive actions they can take.

6. End the circle time on a quiet note by sending a hand hug around the circle. Sit quietly in the circle, holding hands. Gently squeeze the hand of the child next to you, and send the hug from child to child.

## Let's Explore Together

1. It is a good possibility that children will talk about sharing and taking turns. Ask, "How does it feel when it seems like someone is getting more turns than you? What can we do about this?"

2. Show the children the My Turn can you made ahead of time. Give each child a tongue depressor to decorate with her name and some drawings.

3. Explain that you will put all the name sticks in the can. When it is time to choose someone to be the line leader or some other activity, you will reach inside with your eyes closed and choose a name. Then, that name goes out of the can until all the other names have been drawn. Talk about this approach. How is it fair?

4. Invite the children to help you make a list of fair rules for games in the class. The children can brainstorm the rules they think are appropriate and then illustrate them on a sign to hang in the room.

5. Play a Fair Game to practice sharing fairly. Put a collection of small objects in a bag. Have two or three less than needed to give every child five. Pass the bag around, and ask the children to take one object out and pass the bag to the next person. Continue passing the bag around the circle until it is empty. What do they notice? What can they do to make the situation fair? Let the children come up with a solution.

6. Introduce board games to practice taking turns. Games such as Candyland and Chutes and Ladders are good choices. The children may like to invent their own board games.

## Learning Extensions and Building Community

1. Periodically introduce "How would you feel if . . ." questions to your circle-time discussions. These will inspire the children to talk about their feelings and the issues of fairness.

   - How would you feel if I took your toy?
   - How would you feel if someone called you a name?
   - How would you feel if I would not share a toy with you?
   - How would you feel if someone pushed you out of line?

   Each one of these can make a wonderful conversation starter.

2. Extend these conversations to include discussions of what the children can do when someone is upset. Choose one question to discuss, such as the following:

■ What could you say or do to help someone feel better?

■ If someone is frightened, what could you do?

■ What could you do if someone needs help?

■ What could you do if someone looks sad?

Each of these questions can start a lively conversation about conflict resolution.

3. Encourage families to participate in the exploration of fairness. They can talk about family rules and what to do when someone does not follow the rules. Suggest that they play card and board games, which require taking turns and playing fair.

**SEL SPOTLIGHT**

Children are wonderful at using the words you model in the context of an event. When you are monitoring a situation, emphasize words for conflict resolution. Repeat the words many times when talking to the children. This will help them notice the words and begin to use them in a similar context.

# How We've Grown

The year the children spend in your class is filled with many changes and with growth that they can easily recognize. This is a good topic to discuss toward the end of your year with the children. It provides them with the opportunity to reflect on all the things they have learned to do.

### Language Skills:

- Expressive vocabulary
- Creative expression
- Sequencing

### Social-Emotional Skills:

- Self-reflection
- Noticing change
- Sharing

### Materials:

- Photos of the children throughout the year
- Drawing paper
- Markers and crayons
- Glue sticks
- Chart paper or whiteboard
- Camera
- Photos from home (optional)
- Small photo albums

### Ahead of Time:

Invite the families to send in photos of their children from infancy to now.

## Let's Get Involved

1. Start circle time with a song to celebrate the year together. Use these words, sung to the tune of "Sing a Song of Sixpence," or make up your own!

   *Sing a song of children.*
   *Look at how we've grown.*
   *We have made some friends here,*
   *All on our own.*
   *When we get together,*
   *We laugh and sing and play.*
   *Isn't this a happy way*
   *To be throughout the day?*

2. Remind the children that they have all grown this year. They have learned new skills, made new friends, and had fun.

3. Invite the children to reflect on the year, from the first days of school and to now. Ask, "How did you feel when you first came to school? How do you feel now? What changed? What can you do now that you couldn't do in the beginning of the year?"

4. If available, share some photos from the beginning of school. What do the children notice? Ask, "What do you remember doing in this photo?"

Invite the children to talk about how they have grown and changed. Place the photos on a table for the children to explore after circle time.

## Let's Explore Together

1. Children can continue exploring growth and change in your literacy area. If available, look at the school photos together. Invite the children to notice how they have changed.

2. Provide paper and art materials for the children to use to draw self-portraits. Ask the children to tell you about what they notice about themselves and what they can do now. Write their dictation on cards to post in the room.

3. Take photos of the children and how they look now! They may like to create simple picture frames for their photos to display in a "We Have Grown" bulletin-board display.

4. Have the children suggest endings for the sentence, "I have grown and now I can…."

5. Make copies of their self-portraits and their photos for creating a class yearbook. The children will love to get these keepsakes and will delight in having their friends "sign" their pages just like the big kids!

6. Sequence is an important language skill. Have the children work with photos from the year to create a sequence from left to right on the literacy table. There is bound to be some discussion about what happened first, next, and last. When they are done, display the photos on a bulletin board in left-to-right progression. The children will love to visit and revisit them for weeks!

7. If available, have the children make similar timelines of photos with their own personal photos from home. Encourage them to look for the photos of when they were babies and work from there. This is a wonderful activity for building language and vocabulary. The children may like to put their photos together in small, inexpensive photo albums. Invite the children to share their photo books in circle time.

## Learning Extensions and Building Community

1. Families often want to know the words to the songs you sing in school. Invite the children to look back at the year in songs and make a songbook to share with their families. Let them suggest their favorite songs from the year. Sing them together to share the fun of remembering the best of the best. Print the lyrics to their favorites, and ask the children to illustrate.

2. Children love the concept of *best:* The best thing they did in school, the best visitor, the best snack, and the best game. Invite the children to talk about all the "bests" they can remember from the year. Make a "Best of" list!

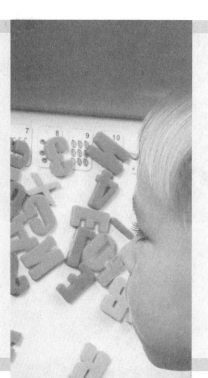

**SEL SPOTLIGHT**
**Young children do not naturally reflect on themselves; they are typically more in the here and now. We can ask them to reflect on very specific activities that have meaning to their lives. Growing and changing is a great place to start because all children want to be big kids. Personalized activities that invite them to think about themselves and their changes build the important skill of self-awareness.**

# Getting to the Heart of Literacy

Children are deeply fascinated by words, letters, and books. Through the world of literacy, children learn about the many forms of writing, communicating, and sharing. They begin to feel comfortable sharing a story or a word with the group and also learn how to listen to what others have to say. The creative aspect of literacy speaks to children's emotional beings and encourages them to express without fear of being wrong.

# Let's Go on a Letter Hunt

Young children are just learning about the beauty and art of letters and words. As they begin to recognize familiar letters in their names, they will notice those letters in their environment, too!

## Literacy Skills:

- Recognizing the letters in their names
- Matching letters to words in the environment
- Tallying the letters found

## Social-Emotional Skills:

- Working with a partner
- Sharing materials
- Helping others
- Sharing in front of a group

## Materials:

- Paper
- Small clipboards or sturdy cardboard, one for each child
- Crayons and markers
- Chart paper or whiteboard

## Ahead of Time:

- Prepare name papers for each child: Write the child's name across the top of a sheet of paper. Draw lines down the paper to make columns underneath each of the letters in the name.
- If you have a child with some unusual letters in her name, be sure to post some simple signs or letter cards in the room and the school with those letters, so that the child has a feeling of success as she looks for the letters in the environment.

## Let's Get Involved

1. Start with your own name in a circle-time gathering. You will inspire the children to join in as you model the activity. You might want to use the name the children call you, or you could introduce your first name. Write your name on a sheet of chart paper or the whiteboard. Tell the children, "These are the letters in my name. Does anyone recognize any of the letters? Let's see which ones we know." Put a tally mark under each letter they can name. Help the children with any difficult letters.

2. Praise the children for their effort to help you: "Good work. You worked together, and you helped me name the letters in my name. Thank you. We are a good team."

3. Tell them, "Now, I need more help!" Invite them to look around the room at signs or books that might have one of the letters from your name on it. Ask, for example, "Can you see the letter *E* anywhere else in the room? Can you help me find it?" Tell them that every time they find a letter from your name, you will put a mark on the chart to show that it was found.

4. Mention how helping each other can be fun and useful. Discuss how people at work or in sports often work together with a partner or team to get things done. As you look at the chart to see how many examples of each letter they found in the classroom, say, "Wow, look at all that we found together. Go team!"

## Let's Explore Together

1. This is a good activity to do over time. It works best with small groups of four to six children. Divide the children into small groups, and let the first group join you in the literacy center. The rest of the class can explore the other centers until it is their group's turn.

2. Invite the children to pick a partner, or choose one for them. Young children often have trouble with choosing partners, so it can be simpler to think ahead to which children would work best together and make your teams using this knowledge. You can model making partnerships in a very simple and nonthreatening way.

3. Give each child her own personal name paper. Provide clipboards or other surfaces to support their sheets as they carry them around during the hunt. Tell the children that they will go on a letter hunt to find the letters in their names. Show the children how to make a line or a tally mark under a letter on the sheet when they find it in the room.

4. Send the children off hunting around the room, under your watchful eyes. If they need a bit of help to get started, you can choose a child and do the first letter of his name. "Does anyone see the letter *R* in the room? *R* for *Ricky*. Yes! How many do we find? Let's mark it."

5. Let the children hunt, and then gather the teams in the literacy center to share what they found. This activity is not just about finding letters but about working together. Celebrate and emphasize specific cooperative interactions that you see: "Karen, I like the way you showed Ricky where you saw the letter *R.*" "Terrey, I like the way you shared your marker with Jessie."

## Learning Extensions and Building Community

1. Celebrate the letter-hunt partners at a group gathering. Introduce the partners, and ask them to share about their hunt. They can point to several places where they found the letters. Bringing this experience back to the group encourages children to develop the social skill of sharing in front of a group.

2. Over time, expand the letter hunt to the rest of the school and even the neighborhood.

3. For younger children, it might work best for the pair to choose one name to do at a time and then trade. This gives them fewer letters to look for at one time.

**SEL SPOTLIGHT**
Young children are just learning how to share, and sometimes sharing an activity can be even more challenging than sharing a toy or material. Give children opportunities to work together in pairs. You will begin to see your natural leaders and followers. Watch to see whether or not one child is dominating the other rather than simply being helpful. Also, watch the response of the other child. Some children are more followers than leaders and may be happy with all the direction and help!

4. Invite parent involvement by turning this into a shared family activity. Families can take the letter hunt to a much larger experience at the store, at the library, or in the car. This makes a great travel game. Parents just need to set up name boards for each family member and then work together to hunt and find!

# Meet Our Special Friends

The process of getting to know more about each other is one of the best ways to build community and understanding. This activity strengthens expressive language, vocabulary, and letter skills. What better topic to talk about than us?

## Literacy Skills:

- Expressive language
- Vocabulary building
- Recognizing familiar letters and words

## Social-Emotional Skills:

- Asking questions
- Supporting each other
- Communicating ideas in a group
- Giving compliments
- Building empathy

## Materials:

- Chart paper or whiteboard
- Drawing paper
- Crayons and marker
- Photos from home
- Camera (optional)

## Let's Get Involved

This activity starts in your circle time but can go on for days into your activity times. If the children are enjoying the process, you can add to their profiles throughout the year.

1. Bring in a photo of yourself doing something you really love to do. It could be from a family trip or of you participating in a hobby—anything that will tell the children something about who you are outside of school.

2. Model creating a personal profile by writing your name at the top of the chart paper. Post the photo with your name. You can even write your nickname! The children will be fascinated to know if you have one.

3. Invite the children to ask questions: "What would you like to know about me?" You might have to help the children get going. For example, you could suggest they ask about your family or the kinds of pets you have. They could ask what you like to eat or what you do on the weekend.

4. Add the requested information to the chart, taking your time to point out words and letters they might know.

## Let's Explore Together

1. Over the next several days, invite the children to introduce themselves at a circle time. Choose one child a day to share something about himself. If possible, photograph each child. Children can also bring photos from home.

2. Create a personal profile for each child. This can be done on chart paper or in book form. Encourage the children to ask investigative questions: "Do you have a brother or sister? Do you have pets? Do you have a special name your family calls you?" They can also delve a little deeper by asking questions about the things the child likes to do or places he likes to go.

3. Write the answers on paper for all to see. Focus on any words or letters that might be familiar to the children.

4. During activity time, invite the children to draw pictures to add to their files. They can add drawings of their homes, families, or anything they would like to share.

5. This is a project that can continue all year with additions from the children. Post the profiles in the room, or put them in a class book to read in the literacy center. Do not forget to add to your profile, too. The children will be thrilled to learn more and more about you.

## Learning Extensions and Building Community

1. Model compliments as each child is sharing information and ideas. You might say, "I like your nickname because it makes me smile." "You have a small family like me!" "That is a great-looking cat!" You will be providing the children with the appropriate social words and phrases to support their friends. Be specific—this helps children be clear about what they are complimenting and why!

2. Continue the project throughout the year. When a child has a success, put it in her profile. When a child takes a trip or has a family event such as a new baby, put it in the profile. By adding photos, drawings, and writings over time, you create a dynamic project that shares the growth of the community.

3. Display the personal profiles on a family night. Parents love to see photos and the writings of their children.

# "I'm Sorry" Cards

Perhaps some of the most important words for young children to learn are *please, thank you,* and *I'm sorry.* Knowing when and how to use these words appropriately takes a beautiful combination of language and literacy skills combined with social and emotional skills.

## Literacy Skills:

- Vocabulary building
- Recognizing familiar words and phrases
- Writing

## Social-Emotional Skills:

- Understanding when to apologize
- Using words to resolve conflict
- Building a vocabulary of polite words

## Materials:

- Index cards
- Wrapping paper, old greeting cards, or construction paper
- Crayons and markers
- Old magazines (optional)
- Scissors
- Books with opportunities for characters to apologize, such as *Uh-Oh! I'm Sorry* by Jill Ackerman, *I'm Sorry* by Sam McBratney, *Peanut Butter and Jellyfish* by Jarrett Krosoczka, or *Peter Panda Melts Down* by Artie Bennett

## Ahead of Time:

From old magazines, cut out pictures of situations in which someone could apologize, such as a person knocking over a drink or spilling some food.

## Let's Get Involved

1. Start in your circle time with a novel situation that is bound to get children's attention. Pretend to knock something over, drop something, hold a book upside down, or say goodbye instead of hello. Do anything that could be followed with, "I'm sorry."

2. Invite the children to notice what you said. "Do you notice something about what I am saying today? Why do I keep saying, 'I'm sorry'?" Write the words *I'm sorry* on a whiteboard or chart paper.

3. Encourage the children to share when they have said, "I'm sorry" to someone. Ask how it felt to say it. Did it help? It is important for children to understand that we all make some mistakes, but we can feel better when we admit we did something and genuinely feel sorry.

4. Continue the conversation by using examples of when it is important to apologize. For example, you could apologize when you knock over someone's block building, take someone's toy, or hurt someone's feelings. If available, use pictures from magazines or books to illustrate these situations.

## Let's Explore Together

1. In a small group, talk about when you might need an "I'm sorry" card. The children may be more comfortable in a small group to talk about times they needed to say this. They also may be able to talk about times they wish someone had said it to them. It is important for children to understand that everyone makes mistakes. It is also important to admit it when we do. Be open to children's discussions. This is really the heart of the activity.

2. Ask, "What would happen if we had 'I'm sorry' cards to give away? Let's make some!" Explain that for the next several days the class is going to focus on saying "I'm sorry" whenever they make a mistake. The trick is that you have to really mean it.

3. Write the words *I'm sorry* on a large index card or paper. Post the example in the writing center. Provide index cards and markers for the children to use to create their own cards. They may like to add illustrations to their cards.

4. Encourage the children to use the cards whenever they need to take care of an "oops" or mistake.

## Learning Extensions and Building Community

1. Extend the activity by focusing on *thank you.* When do you need to say thank you to someone? How does it feel when someone thanks you?

2. The children can extend the project and the learning by making thank-you cards, too! Write *thank you* on an index card, and hang it in the writing center. Using old greeting cards or wrapping paper, the children can create thank-you cards. Encourage them to make several so they can give them to many different people.

3. Later on, they can make cards to say, "You're welcome." Help them learn when to use them appropriately.

# Every Card Tells a Story

Greeting cards are a wonderful way to show caring and connection. As a teacher, you likely receive many greeting cards throughout the year. In this heartfelt activity, children will use greeting-card art to create their own stories and cards to share with the group.

## Literacy Skills:

- Storytelling
- Vocabulary building
- Making books

## Social-Emotional Skills:

- Expressing creative ideas
- Communicating feelings
- Taking turns
- Sharing materials

## Materials:

- Safety scissors
- Glue sticks
- Heavy paper or oak tag
- Crayons and markers
- Stapler

## Ahead of Time:

- Invite families to send in used greeting cards they are willing to have cut up. Collect a wide variety of cards for all occasions.
- Cut the fronts of the cards away from the backs.
- Choose two or three cards and envelopes to "send" to the class at circle time.

## Let's Get Involved

1. Children love cards! Introduce the activity in your circle time by sharing a few cards with the children. Be dramatic and show the cards in the envelopes, and invite the children to take turns suggesting who might have sent the cards and what they are about. Guide the children in taking turns and listening to all suggestions equally.

2. After everyone has had a chance to make a suggestion, open the first card. Show the front, and ask the children to use the illustrations to "read" the card. Ask, "What is happening in the card? What do you think the card is for? Is it a birthday card or a holiday card? Can you read any words on the front?" Remind the children to raise their hands if they have an idea instead of shouting it out. Reinforce good listening and turn taking by saying, "I like the way that Tim is raising his hand. I am going to call on him."

3. After many guesses and discussions, read the rest of the card to confirm what it is about. Be sure to commend all of the children's ideas equally. The goal of the introduction to the activity is not to be right but to be creative!

## Let's Explore Together

Take the activity to your writing center where the children can create books using greeting cards.

1. Show the children the greeting cards you have collected. Invite them to explore the images and see which ones they are drawn to.

2. Demonstrate how a few cards can be used as illustrations to tell a story. Have children hand you one card at a time, and use the cards for a short story. For example, you might say, "In the beginning there was a bunny. And then the bunny had a birthday party with balloons." Your story does not have to make sense; just have fun with the images and the words.

3. Invite the children to choose their own cards to start their stories. Encourage them to paste a card on heavy drawing paper or oak tag to create the first page of their books. Ask, "How does your story start?"

4. Continue the process by letting the children choose several more cards to paste on separate pages to extend their stories.

5. Emphasize the process of taking turns as you invite the children to "read" their cards to the others at the table. Reinforce listening and waiting skills as the children give their full attention to the "reader."

6. Complete the books by writing the children's dictation on the bottom of each page of their story books.

## Learning Extensions and Building Community

1. Extend the practice with listening and taking turns by having a storytelling or book-sharing time at the end of the day. Invite one or two children to "read" their books to the group. Invite the children to offer compliments on the stories and the art.

2. Set up a special section in your library area to display the books. Call it Every Card Tells a Story. Direct families to the area when they come to visit, so that they can share in the stories, too.

3. The children may like to take their books home for a while and return them to the library after sharing them with their families.

# Create a Class Care Center

Transform your writing center into a care center where the children can create caring messages to share with friends and family.

## Literacy Skills:

- Dictating and/or writing words
- Illustrating ideas
- Learning words for caring and helping

## Social-Emotional Skills:

- Caring for others
- Learning how to show you care
- Asking for help from an adult
- Understanding how to help others

## Materials:

- Index cards
- Drawing paper
- Crayons and markers
- Collage materials
- Glue sticks
- Paper, cut into 1-yard lengths, one for each child

## Ahead of Time:

Surprise the children by redecorating the writing center! Add a sign that says "Caring Center" to the area, and provide picture instructions for creating caring cards and materials. For example, you can neatly print cards that say, "I care," and "I love you." You can also add an example of hug coupons.

## Let's Get Involved

1. In your circle time, start a conversation about caring. Start by telling the children that you care about them. Sing the following to the tune of "The Farmer in the Dell."

   *I care for all of you.*
   *I care for all of you.*
   *Judy, Joseph, Brianna, John,* (add children's names)
   *I care for all of you.* (act out a hug)

   Sing the song several times, making sure to add every child's name. You can point to each child as you say her name.

2. Ask the children, "How do you know when someone cares for you?" Encourage them to brainstorm all the ways they can think of. It might help to suggest people, such as family members or friends, who care about them. This may help them be more specific. This is a good conversation to have over time. Each time you revisit the concept of caring, the children will gain a deeper understanding.

3. Use favorite literature to illustrate caring and examples of caring actions from the classroom.. Show an example of a caring note. It could be a real one, or you can make one up to share. Ask, "Have you ever gotten a surprise card or note from your family or a friend? It feels good to know that someone cares."

4. Suggest the idea of creating a care center in the classroom. The children may have already discovered how you transformed the writing center and will be curious to learn more about it! Tell them, "We are going to change our writing center into a care center. We can go there to write caring notes and hug coupons to share with our friends."

## Let's Explore Together

1. Have you ever noticed how many young children like to make others feel good? That natural generosity is a gift to all. It is a delight to see their faces light up when they create and give little notes to a friend or family member. Invite a small group of children to visit the care center.

2. Ask them to use observation and print-awareness skills to "read" what is available there for them to do. Point to one of the signs, and ask the children to guess what it might say. They may recognize the words *love* or *I*.

3. Show them the materials available for making care cards. This can be a collection of collage and drawing materials. Encourage them to think about whom they would like to make a card for: "Do you know someone who is sad right now or someone who has been sick? You can make that person a card!"

4. Let them create cards for friends or family.

5. Another day, introduce the concept of hug coupons to the care center. These are fun to make, give, and receive. Show the children how to trace their hands (facing out) on each end of a one-yard-long piece of paper. Show them how to draw lines to connect the hands to make a big hug.

6. The children can cut the hugs out, decorate them, and give them to friends who need a hug. Wrap yourself up in the hug—it is big enough!

## Learning Extensions and Building Community

1. Periodically discuss the activities in the care center at a circle time. Invite the children to share what they are working on and how it feels to make a card or coupon. Some children may like to share how it feels to receive one.

2. Over time, you can add additional items to the care center. For example, you might include examples of help coupons that the children can make for their family and friends. They can use the coupons to offer to help with small tasks around the house or at school.

# Our Community Mailboxes

Children will enjoy creating a sense of belonging in the group by making mailboxes where they can receive cards and notes. This will also place a focus on learning how to write their names and the names of their friends!

## Literacy Skills:

- Recognizing their own names and the names of friends
- Writing names
- "Reading" images to decipher words

## Social-Emotional Skills:

- Developing a sense of belonging
- Making self-directed choices
- Seeing self as a member of a group

## Materials:

- Hanging shoe bag with enough pockets for each child to have one
- Photo of each child
- Index cards
- Large nametag stickers
- Small clothespins or stapler
- Marker
- Glue or tape

## Ahead of Time:

- Take photos of the children, and glue or tape one photo on each index card.
- Write the children's names on nametag stickers.

## Let's Get Involved

1. Bring your collection of children's photos to circle time for a community-building activity. Start with the first photo and sing the following lyrics to the tune of "Frère Jacques":

   *Who is this friend?*
   *Who is this friend?*
   *Can you name who it is?*

   *Point to our special friend.*
   *Point to our special friend.*
   *There he is.*
   *There he is!*

2. Give each child her photo to hold after you finish her verse of the song.
3. When each child has her photo and has heard her verse of the song, sing a final verse. Encourage the children to proudly show their photos to the group.

   *Where are our friends?*
   *Where are our friends?*
   *Show me yours, way up high.*
   *We are all together.*
   *We all play together*
   *In our class,*
   *In our class.*

4. Explain that this week the class will be using the photos and name labels to make mailboxes for sharing cards and notes with class friends. The social-emotional learning in this activity is subtler than some other activities. You could ask the children how it felt to have their photo recognized, but many will not be able to verbalize more than saying it felt "good." Trust that the process of being noticed is enough to build important community-building and identity skills. Sometimes we do not have to talk about it as much as experience it!

## Let's Explore Together

Work with small groups at a time to practice recognizing names and to create mailboxes.

1. Place a few of the name labels on the table, and invite the children to guess the name for each one. It is helpful to just start with two or three so there is not too much distraction. This is not a test but an opportunity to see what names they are familiar with.

2. The children may like to match the photos with the correct names. Mix the photo cards and nametags up, and let them match them. Each time you do this fun game, the children will be making a richer connection to the words and photos.

3. Show the children how to use a small clothespin to attach their photo to the top of a pocket. If you want something more permanent, you can use a stapler to attach it for them with their help.

4. Ask the children to attach their sticker nametags to the front of their pocket.

5. Once everyone has a mailbox, encourage the children to make cards or messages to send to friends! Often children ask a teacher how to spell a friend's name. With the mailbox system, the children will have all they need right in front of them. Point out how they can find a friend's photo and then see how to copy her name. Simple!

6. As they work on their notes, ask, "What would you like to say to a friend? Do you want to write words or send a picture? Do not forget to look on her mailbox to see how to spell her name!"

## Learning Extensions and Building Community

1. Remember to place notes from you in their mailboxes frequently. Even at this young age, children are very aware of who is getting mail and who is not.

2. Play a game once a week in which the children draw a name and image from a bowl to find their secret friend! They can draw a picture or write a note and sneak it into their friend's mailbox.

3. Surprise the children by inviting parents to send in notes or cards to add to the mailboxes.

4. Extend the activity in the mailbox center over time by introducing envelopes and even child-designed stamps! Add shaped paper cutouts that fit your theme to extend the fun. Use animals, geometric shapes, symbols, or just unusual shapes to pique the children's interest and creativity.

**SEL SPOTLIGHT**

There is something so magical when children realize that they can make their own choices and be successful. Often the delight registers in their eyes, and the children's interest in an activity can skyrocket. When this activity is in place and the children know how to use the mailbox, pictures, and name cues, they are on their own! The self-confidence and independence that is fostered is essential to later school success.

# This Is Me in Five Lines!

Developing a sense of identity within the group is an essential part of social and emotional growth. Combine it with literacy learning by encouraging the children to work cooperatively to create poems.

## Materials:

- Chart paper or whiteboard
- Drawing paper
- Crayons and markers
- Index cards
- Basket
- Camera (optional)
- Photo album (optional)

### Literacy Skills:

- Discovering parts of speech
- Recognizing names and words
- Dictating and "reading" expressive words
- Book knowledge

### Social-Emotional Skills:

- Seeing self as a member of the group
- Learning about each other
- Building self-esteem
- Developing self-awareness
- Helping others

## Ahead of Time:

- Create your own cinquain as a model for the children, and write the poem out on chart paper.

  *Ellen*

  *Happy Bouncy*

  *Reading, Swimming, Dancing*

  *Ready to go!*

  *Ellen*

  - ✦ First line is a noun (your name)
  - ✦ Second line is two adjectives to describe yourself
  - ✦ Third line is three action words to describe what you like to do
  - ✦ Fourth line is any phrase to describe you
  - ✦ Fifth line is a noun again
- Write the children's names on index cards, and place the cards facedown in a basket.

## Let's Get Involved

1. A cinquain is a traditional five-line poem format that can give children a structure for their writing. It is customarily used with names. Introduce your own cinquain in a circle time. This will provide both an example and an inspiration to children to create their own. Introduce the poem by saying, "Guess what I did last night? I wrote a poem, and it's about me! Do you want to hear it?"

2. Show the poem to the children, and invite them to see if they recognize any of the words. They might know your name or some of the adjectives and verbs.

3. Invite them to notice the first and last lines. "Do you notice any words written twice? What do you see?" Help the children notice that the first and last lines are the same—your name!

4. Read the poem and talk about how it describes you. Invite the children to reflect on the words you chose. "Do you think my words describe me? Am I bouncy and happy? Did you know I like to swim?"

5. Tell the children that they will work together to create poems for each other.

## Let's Explore Together

This activity works best in small groups in your literacy area.

1. Bring your poem to the table to use as a model. Set the basket of names on the table.
2. Invite a child to draw a card. The name on it is the first name to use in a cinquain.
3. On chart paper or the whiteboard, write the poem as the children create it. Start with the first line: the child's name.
4. The next line is two words to describe the child. Encourage the children to brainstorm a list of words to describe their friend. Then, the child can choose the best ones for the poem. Write the words she chooses on the chart as the second line.
5. The third line is three words to describe actions that the child likes to do. Ask the child what activities she enjoys. Suggest that the child can invite friends to help think of activities, too. Write the words on the chart.
6. The fourth line is just something to say about the child. Encourage the child to ask her friends for help if she cannot think of anything.
7. Write the child's name again as the fifth line. Once the poem is complete, read it together!
8. Continue until each child has a cinquain.
9. If desired, put out art materials for the children to use to decorate the edges of their poems or draw self-portraits to accompany them.</NL>

## Learning Extensions and Building Community

1. Extend the learning by creating a class book of the cinquain poems. Put this together in a large photo album to protect the poems during multiple "reads."
2. It can be fun to use a camera to create "selfies" to illustrate the book, too.
3. Introduce another five-line poem style: lanterne, which works with the number of syllables:
   - Choose a one-syllable word for the first line.
   - Choose two words or syllables for the second line.
   - Choose three words or syllables for the third line.
   - Choose four words or syllables for the fourth line.
   - The last line is one syllable again.

| |
|---|
| Kay |
| Bouncy |
| Full of fun! |
| Ready to go! |
| Smile |

4. It is important for children to be able to share something about their friends in school when they are back at home. Set up a schedule for sending the cinquain book home once a week. Provide pages in the book for the families to write their responses to the poems and pictures!

5. Let the children draw portraits of their friends for their poems. This is another delightful way for children to help each other. Create an art and poetry show of the poems and portraits, and ask families and friends to come!

**SEL SPOTLIGHT**

Young children often want to help each other, but they may not always know the best way to do it. Giving children specific tasks that they can do successfully gives them an understanding of what helping really looks like. Often, helping is very practical with activities such as cleanup, setting the table, or being line leader. This activity shows children how they can creatively help a friend—collaboration at its best!

# My Face Shows It

Children often equate facial expressions with feelings. You can use this simple handmade book as a springboard to discussions about feelings.

### Literacy Skills:

- Book knowledge
- Small-motor coordination
- Vocabulary building

### Social-Emotional Skills:

- Recognizing emotions
- Expressing emotions
- Using feelings vocabulary
- Listening
- Following directions

## Let's Get Involved

1. Invite the children to read the emotions in a variety of facial expressions that you make. Use expressions that the children may be familiar with. Choose one, and ask them to say how you are feeling. Ask them how they know that is how you are feeling.

2. Encourage them to suggest very specific words for your expression. Write their words on chart paper. Next to each word, draw a face to show what emotion the word goes with.

3. Challenge them with a few complicated expressions, too. Try shy, excited, or nervous!

4. If there is time, extend the conversation by exploring facial expressions in favorite children's books or in magazine photos.

## Let's Explore Together

1. Using a blank paper plate, show the children how you can draw a feeling on the face of the plate.

2. Give the children paper plates, and encourage them to draw different feelings on several plates using the circle of the plate as the head shape.

3. Encourage them to talk about the feelings they are drawing. If the children need assistance, you can model feelings words for them.

4. Tell them that they will combine their feelings faces to create feelings books. Encourage them to make a front and back cover for their books.

5. Show them how to stack their feelings plates, line up the holes you punched ahead of time, and tie the plates together (or use the brass brads) to form a book. The children can work in pairs to help each other bind their books.

6. Take a photo of each child to print out and glue on the cover. They can make any face they want for the cover!

7. Ask the children to add their names and book titles to the covers if they like.

## Learning Extensions and Building Community

1. Encourage the children to share their books with others at a circle time, but remind them that no one is required to share his book. Some children may like to tell a story using their books or share a bit about the faces in their books.

2. Add a song! Use the tune of "If You're Happy And You Know It" to experiment with different facial expressions for emotions. Add all the ones the children use in their books.

**SEL SPOTLIGHT**
Young children can have difficulty talking about feelings. They often do not have the vocabulary to express their emotions in words. Drawing is an accessible and often successful outlet for expressing feelings and can get the conversation started.

# Fun with Initials and Names

Even though they may not be writing their full names yet, young children love to work with the first letters of their names. Not only does this develop visual discrimination, but it also enhances self-concept and self-esteem.

**Literacy Skills:**

- Initial letters
- Initial letter sounds
- Matching

**Social-Emotional Skills:**

- Developing self-awareness
- Seeing self as a member of a group
- Focusing

**Materials:**

- Alphabet chart
- Index cards
- Markers
- Drawing paper
- Tempera paint
- Paintbrushes
- Collage materials
- Oak tag
- Glue
- Clay or playdough
- Plastic letters

**Ahead of Time:**

- Make an initial card for the first letter of each child's name, and make one for you, too!
- Draw a thick outline of a giant initial for each child on a large sheet of oak tag.

## Let's Get Involved

1. Show an initial card for your name. Use the name that the children are familiar with. You can introduce it with a song sung to the tune of "The Alphabet Song."

   *A-B-C-D-E-F-G*
   *Which letter is so special for me?*
   *If you look, you will see*
   *My name starts with the letter E!*

2. Point to the alphabet chart, and show where your initial letter is in the alphabet. Hold the card up to match the letters together.

3. Now introduce the letter cards for the children. This is a good way to involve cooperation and turn-taking skills. Ask, "Would you like to see the cards for all our friends? I have one for each of you. I will hold one up; see if you recognize it. Do you know anyone whose name starts with the sound and letter of *B*? Yes, Beth! Let's sing the song for Beth."

4. Encourage sharing in the group by inviting each child to stand up to show the card and demonstrate tracing the letter on the card and in the air. "Can you make the shape of Beth's letter?"

5. Continue in this manner until each child has an initial card.

6. Invite the children to match their cards on the alphabet chart. "Can you find where your letter is in the alphabet? Is it in the beginning, at the end, or in the middle?" Help them if they need it.

## Let's Explore Together

Each time a child makes something with his initial, he develops both literacy and social skills. He begins to recognize the letter and also sees a symbol that represents who he is.

1. Invite a small group of children to the literacy area. Show the oak tag papers with the outlined initials. Ask the children to find the one that represents their name. Some children who may be more aware of letters can help others find their letters. Celebrate helping by thanking them.

2. Provide tempera paint and brushes for the children to use to paint their oak tag letters. Do not worry if they go over the lines. The letters will get cut out later.

3. After the letters are dry, cut them out and provide collage materials that the children can use to decorate their letters.

4. Encourage the children to share their initial art at the next circle time. The class can sing the song with each letter!

5. Put out clay or playdough at another table for the children to experiment with making letters. Show the children how to roll a piece of clay to make a rope and then shape it into a letter. Put out plastic letters for children to use as models, or they can press the plastic letters into the clay to make letter imprints.

6. Apply the initials to the classroom. The children can make simple folded place cards for snack time. They can decorate a card that has their letter on it. Fold it in half so it can stand up at their place at the table. "Can you find your initial? That is where you sit!"

## Learning Extensions and Building Community

1. Play a group game with the alphabet chart and the initial cards. Have the children look on the chart to find their letters, then ask each child to stand in front of her initial. All the *A*s go first, and then the *B*s, and so on.

2. After everyone is lined up in front of a letter, look at the graph they have created. Ask, "Which letter do we have the most of? Are there any letters that we do not have as an initial in our room?"

3. Make initial-letter puzzles. After children have enjoyed their oak tag letter creations for a while, they can turn them into their very own puzzles. Show the children how to cut each letter into three simple pieces and then put it together again!

4. Outside on the playground, make a hopscotch board using initials. Use playground chalk to make a grid, and write the children's initials in the boxes. Play traditional hopscotch, or make up your own rules.

# Making Wish Flags for the World

How do we make a wish for the world? With words, art, and heart! Children will enjoy this special dissolving art technique for making wish flags to hang out on the playground.

## Literacy Skills:

- Verbalizing thoughts and feelings
- Dictating words
- Drawing images to represent words and feelings

## Social-Emotional Skills:

- Expressing caring and concern
- Feeling empathy
- Brainstorming ideas
- Thinking about others in the world

## Materials:

- Chart paper or whiteboard
- Paper coffee filters
- Washable markers
- String
- Clothespins
- Photos from magazines or books of people and places around the world
- Recording of the song "It's a Small World" (optional)

## Ahead of Time:

Tie the string on a fence or between two poles or trees outside.

## Let's Get Involved

1. Begin circle time with a song. You can use "It's a Small World," or try these lyrics sung to the tune of "Row, Row, Row Your Boat."

   *Wish, wish, make a wish.*
   *Send it to the world.*
   *Merrily, merrily, happily, happily*
   *Wishes to the world.*

2. Start a conversation about the world—it is both small and big. Show the children some photos of people and places. Encourage the children to express what they notice about the photos. There may be particular images that interest the children and get them talking about similarities to and differences from them and their own world.

3. Use the photos of people to invite the children to suggest how the people in the photos might be feeling. "What might they be feeling or wishing? How would you feel if you were in this place?"

4. Tell the children, "Today we are going to be making wish flags to hang outside and send out to our beautiful, small world. What happens when you make a wish on a birthday cake? You blow out the candles, and

the flame goes away, taking your wish with it. We are going to write and draw our wishes on the flags with washable markers. When we hang the flags outside, the rain and sun will dissolve the colors and send the wishes out to the world!

## Let's Explore Together

1. Work with small groups in your writing and literacy center to brainstorm words to write on their wish flags. Write a few words on chart paper or the whiteboard, such as *happy, friendly, love,* and *peace.* Ask, "Do you know any of these words? I can read them to you. These are words we might want other people in the world to feel. What would you want your family and friends to feel? How would they feel if they had everything that they needed?"

2. Encourage the children to suggest words to add to the board. Remind them that what they want—happiness, safety, friends, love—is often what others want, too. Be supportive of all ideas, understanding that this may be the first time the children have talked about the needs and wishes of others.

3. Go over the list, and ask the children to choose their favorite word or words to use on their flags.

4. Give the children the coffee filters and markers. Show them how they can press the paper down to make it flatter and easier to write and draw on.

5. Encourage them to write any or all of the words on the chart and to add drawings to their flags. Provide plenty of papers; often children want to do more than one. Remind the children that the flags are "magic" because when the sun and rain touches their flags, the words and drawings will dissolve and send their wishes to the world just like the flame of a birthday candle.

6. Toward the end of the session, invite the children to show their flags to another child and tell about it.

7. Show the children how to clip a clothespin on their flags.

## Learning Extensions and Building Community

1. If possible, have a sharing time in a circle before taking the flags outside. The children may like to hold up their flags to share their wishes.

2. Music has a way of bringing our hearts and minds together. Sing the "Make a Wish" song as the children march outside.

3. Show the children how to clip their flags on a string strung low enough for them to reach. Or, they can use their clothespins to attach their wishes to a tree, bush, or fence.

4. Periodically, gather the group in the playground to check on the wishes to see if the words and art have totally dissolved yet. The more they dissolve, the more wishes are sent! Celebrate when a flag is fully clear. Wishes sent!

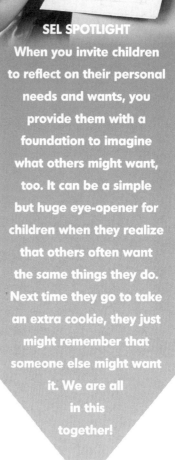

**SEL SPOTLIGHT**
When you invite children to reflect on their personal needs and wants, you provide them with a foundation to imagine what others might want, too. It can be a simple but huge eye-opener for children when they realize that others often want the same things they do. Next time they go to take an extra cookie, they just might remember that someone else might want it. We are all in this together!

# Getting to the Heart of Motor Skills

## CHAPTER 6

Perhaps more than any other curriculum area, motor activities are the basis for building social cooperation, turn taking, and helping skills. Many of these activities need a partner or a group to be successful, and this makes for a natural bridge between motor and social skills. Children build self-confidence as they master both their small- and large-motor abilities. Who does not feel thrilled when she learns to snap her fingers or hop on one foot? Let's explore motor skills together.

# Obstacle Circus

Children are just learning about their senses of space and place. Movement activities that invite them to use their bodies to explore their space build both motor and social skills.

**Motor Skills:**

- Cross-lateral movement
- Spatial relationships
- Gross motor skills
- Problem solving

**Social-Emotional Skills:**

- Following the rules
- Taking turns
- Supporting each other

**Materials:**

- Objects for an obstacle course, such as boxes, pillows, sheets, blocks, hoops, and carpet squares
- Books or photos of the circus
- Balls or beach balls
- Circus-themed music

## Let's Get Involved

1.  The spatial relationships of *up, down, next to, between,* and so on are wonderful concepts for helping children develop a sense of space and place in the world. Play with this topic in a circus theme. Sing the following lyrics to the tune of "I've Been Working on the Railroad":

    *I've been playing at the circus*
    *All the livelong day.*
    *I've been playing at the circus*
    *Just to pass the time away.*
    *See the horses prance lightly,*
    *    jump up, and walk all around.*
    *See the clowns dancing in and out,*
    *    making a big sound.*

2.  Talk about the circus, and if possible, read a book about it. Ask the children what they know about the circus: What happens there? What can you see at the circus?

3.  Play a quick cooperative game to get the children involved with the theme and each other. Ask the children to stand up and stand in front of a friend. Tell them they are going to be clowns together. Give each pair of children a beach ball to balance between them. They can use their tummies to hold it. Challenge them to stand back-to-back or shoulder-to-shoulder and put the ball between them. Notice the children's ability to work together to solve the problems.

4. Tell the children that you will work together to create a circus obstacle course.

## Let's Explore Together

1. An obstacle course is the perfect tool for exploring spatial concepts. Involve the children in constructing the course—this helps them focus on creating the spaces as well as moving through them. Hands-on learning at its best! Show the children the materials you have collected and invite them to suggest how to place them around the space to create a circus path. If they need prompting, ask, "What can we use to crawl in? What can we use to crawl under? What can we climb over?"

2. Encourage the children to try different combinations of objects to make the obstacle course.
   - **Over:** Use large blocks or piles of pillows.
   - **Under:** Use a sheet or blanket draped over a rope.
   - **Through:** Lay a ladder, a row of plastic hoops, or carpet squares flat on the floor.
   - **In:** Use a large cardboard box.
   - **Around:** Use chairs in a staggered line or large blocks arranged in a zigzag pattern.

3. When the children are satisfied with their obstacle course, talk about following the rules for the game. Explain that the rules will keep them safe as they travel the circus path together. Only one child will go through the course at a time. Ask the children to sit in a line along the edge of the path and cheer for the child going through. Then, the next child takes a turn.

4. Put on some fun circus music and encourage the children to crawl through the obstacle course. As they go through, emphasize the words for spatial relationships as the children embody them. "You are going over the pillows. You are crawling under the blanket." This will help reinforce both the physical and language experience.

5. Try it again, this time encouraging the children to walk through the course. How is it different?

6. For a greater challenge, let the children cross-crawl through the course. This movement encourages children to begin to cross the midline of the body, causing both hemispheres of the brain to work together.

## Learning Extensions and Building Community

1. Suggest that the families create their own obstacle courses at home. They can have fun crawling over, under, and through together!

2. Repeat the activity frequently. Each time the children create the obstacle course, it will be different and will encourage motor problem solving.

3. Revisit the rules of the game. Ask the children to suggest why they think rules are important for an active game.

**SEL Spotlight**
Young children need clear rules to help them understand what is expected of them in an activity. An obstacle course is perfect because there is a beginning and an end and very clear stages throughout. This helps children feel confident that they are following the rules.

# Wait, Please!

Young children are constantly on the go, and they can find it challenging to stop and wait. The mind-body connection is a powerful one for young children. They can learn to incorporate many skills by experiencing them with their bodies. Help them practice waiting and stopping with fun movement games.

**Motor Skills:**
- Gross motor
- Hand movements
- Balance
- Starting and stopping
- Physical problem solving

**Social-Emotional Skills:**
- Waiting
- Listening
- Reflecting

**Materials:**
- Recorded music in a wide variety of genres
- Two 9" x 12" card stock pieces
- Markers

**Ahead of Time:**

Draw a red light on one 9" x 12" card and a green light on the other.

## Let's Get Involved

1. Share a personal story with the children about having to wait for something. Perhaps you were waiting in line at the grocery store or waiting for dinner to be ready. Talk about how it feels to have to stop and wait.

2. Ask the children to talk about waiting. Sometimes we have to wait a turn, or sometimes we have to stop and wait to be safe. Ask, "When do we have to wait at school?" "When do you have to wait at home?" "How does it feel to wait? Can it be hard to wait sometimes?"

3. Introduce a fun song that illustrates the concept of waiting, sung to the tune of "The Farmer in the Dell."

   *Wait a minute, please.* (hold up one finger)
   *Wait a minute, please.* (hold up one finger)
   *Stop, wait, and clasp your hands.* (hold up a hand, palm out)
   *Wait a minute, please.* (clasp hands together)

4. You can add verses for different situations. For example, the children can "stop, wait, and look around" when they need to be safe. Or, they can "stop, look, and wait your turn." Invite the children to make up hand movements to illustrate each line.

5. Invite the children to brainstorm a list of times they need to wait in school. Post these on a "Wait a Minute" board.

## Let's Explore Together

1. There are many games that let children practice starting, stopping, and waiting. Gather the children together in an open space where they can move freely.

2. Ask them to sit in a circle to discuss the rules of the game before you play it. This will reinforce the concept of waiting and will help them know what is expected of them. "We are going to play a stop-and-go game. When I play the music, you can move around with any movement you like. When the music stops, you have to stop and wait. Listen again, and you will find out what to do when the music starts again."

3. Ask the children to find a place where they can move without bumping into another child. A great way to illustrate this is to invite them to imagine that they are umbrellas and to put their arms partially out and do a spin. If they do not bump someone, they have plenty of room!

4. Put on music, and join them in moving around. After a couple of minutes, sneak away and stop the music. Say, "Stop. Wait."

5. Remind the children to freeze in place in whatever movement they were making. Be prepared for some giggles as the children look around and see the fun shapes they have frozen in.

6. Play the music again, but this time offer the children a direction for their movement. For example, they can hop, slide, crawl, or tiptoe to the music.

7. Continue the game, occasionally stopping the music. When the children stop and wait, they can look around at the movements the other children are frozen in. On the last turn, end the game with the direction, "Stop, wait, and sit down."

8. After the game, talk about how it felt to stop and wait. "Was it hard to wait and listen for directions? Was it fun?"

## Learning Extensions and Building Community

1. Play Stop and Wait frequently. Try letting the children pair up for more social interaction. When the music stops, the children can find a partner to wait with. Then, when the music starts, the pairs can move together! Each time the music stops, let them add a partner until the entire class is moving together in one big group. Then, stop for one big group wait!

2. Play the game outside using the shadows in the playground. Invite the children to notice their shadows as they move. When the music stops,

encourage them to pause and make a fun shadow shape with their bodies. Do it again and again!

3.  Play the classic game of Red Light, Green Light. It is the perfect game for practicing starting and stopping. Ask the children to stand in a line in front of the leader. The leader holds up the green-light card and says, "Green light," to let the children move forward. When the leader holds up the red-light card and says, "Red light," they have to stop. This is a good game for waiting for directions.

**SEL SPOTLIGHT**
Games that exaggerate the process of waiting help children better understand what it feels like to stop and wait. Studies have shown that when you have children exaggerate a behavior, they become more focused on what is being asked of them. Waiting is a great play activity because children love the concept of freezing and waiting.

# Balls, Balls, Balls!

Young children love to play with balls of all sizes and types. They are the perfect props for exploring both small- and large-motor skills.

## Materials:

- Balls in a variety of sizes and materials
- Gallon jugs
- Masking or colored tape
- Balloons
- Large plastic hoops
- Scrap paper
- Umbrella
- Plastic garbage bag
- Paper
- Marker
- Liquid tempera paint
- Cardboard boxes

## Motor Skills:

- Rolling
- Bouncing
- Throwing
- Catching
- Eye-hand coordination
- Problem solving

## Social-Emotional Skills:

- Focusing
- Following the rules
- Supporting each other

## Ahead of Time:

- Make catching scoops out of gallon containers. Cut the bottom few inches off the jug, and cover the edges with masking or colored tape. The children can hold the handle and use the open end to scoop up balls.
- Write a numeral from one to nine on a sheet of paper with a marker. Make one sheet for each numeral.
- Blow up the balloons, and have them ready to go in a plastic garbage bag.

## Let's Get Involved

1. As soon as you show up at circle time with a ball in your hand, you will have the children's focused attention. Ask the children to take turns greeting each other by rolling a ball. Model the game by saying, "I am going to roll the ball to someone to say hello. Watch and listen. Rolling, rolling, rolling to you, Tom. Good morning, Tom!" Roll the ball to that child.

2. Let that child then say, "Rolling, rolling, rolling to you," and choose a child to roll the ball to as he says that friend's name. Continue until each child has had a turn.

3. Children may get excited about the ball and try to grab it. Remind them that only the person whose name is called may reach for the ball, and everybody else must keep his bottom on the rug. After the game, talk about why it is important for only one person to catch the ball at a time.

4. Ball-rolling games are a wonderful addition to your circle time. You can build both motor and thinking skills by changing the topic each time you play. For example, try doing a quick thinking game. The person with the ball asks a question, such as "What is your favorite color?" and then rolls the ball to someone in the group. The person who catches it offers an answer and then rolls the ball to someone else. Try to keep the ball moving so the children have to think and move quickly.

## Let's Explore Together

There are so many ways to play with balls. You can use them both inside and outside to build small- and large-muscle skills as well as thinking and problem solving. Here are a few games to try.

1. Use the scoops to play a preschool version of the game jai alai. This game works best in a large open area or outdoors because the children are just learning the coordination skills for catching and throwing. Their aim is not too good yet! Pair the children or break them into small groups.

2. Have them stand in front of each other or in a small circle and take turns putting the ball in the scoop and tossing it to a friend. Keep the children fairly close to each other at first. This way there is less space they have to cover with their throw. Eventually they can back up and try it from a greater distance.

3. Lay large plastic hoops on the floor or ground for the children to use to experiment with bouncing. Put a number in each hoop, and ask the children to bounce their ball that many times in the hoop before they move on to the next one. They may need practice bouncing a ball inside a hoop before they can bounce and count with any accuracy.

4. Umbrella basketball is a great rainy-day game to play with children. Show them how to crumple a piece of paper into a ball very tightly. Place an open umbrella upside down on the floor, and ask the children to try to make a basket by tossing the paper ball into the umbrella.

## Learning Extensions and Building Community

1. Extend the learning into a cooperative game by switching from balls to balloons! Invite the children to work together to try to keep the balloons up in the air. Add a challenge by inviting them to keep the balloons up in the air without using their hands!

2. Balls are also excellent for math and movement. Use balls of all different sizes on your playground slide for a rolling estimating activity. Ask the children to guess which of the balls will roll the fastest down the slide. Which will roll the slowest? How far away will a ball fly off the bottom?

3. Extend the focus on balls and eye-hand coordination by using balls to make paintings. Place paper inside a cardboard box with high sides. Provide small balls dipped in paint for the children to carefully roll around to make a painting.

**SEL SPOTLIGHT**
Happily, balls are so engaging that they make an excellent focusing device. Help the children understand the importance of focusing by verbalizing what they are doing. "I can see you are really focusing on the ball, Janie. I can see you are paying attention so that it goes in the basket."

# Do the Opposite

The concept of *opposite* can be challenging for children to think about. But when you give them movement experiences with opposites, children begin to build a mind-body awareness of the topic.

**Motor Skills:**

- Walking
- Jumping
- Reaching
- Eye-hand coordination
- Problem solving

**Social-Emotional Skills:**

- Following directions
- Listening to the leader
- Being the leader

**Materials:**

- Recorded music
- Newspaper
- Tape
- Stickers

**Ahead of Time:**

Prepare a follow-the-leader hat. This can be a silly paper party hat or a folded newspaper hat. Decorate it with fun stickers.

## Let's Get Involved

1.  Use your circle time to do small-motor opposites activities. Start with an opposites storytelling game. Invite the children to share in telling a story using the format of the "We're Going on a Bear Hunt" story game. Tell the children you need their help to tell a story. "I am going to tell a story, and you will be adding movements and sounds to go with it. Can you help me?"

2.  Ask the children to tap a beat on their legs. Let them practice the beat first. "Can you tap a slow beat?" "Can you tap a fast beat?" "Slow." "Fast."

3.  Tell the story.

    *Once upon a time, Little Fox was walking slowly through the forest.* (slow tap)

    *As he walked around, he heard something up in a tree. He pointed to it* (look up and point)

    *But, there was nothing there.*

    *He went back to walking slowly through the forest.* (slow tap)

    *This time he thought he heard something down in a hole in a log.*

    *He stopped, looked down, and pointed.* (look down and point)

    *Oh my! What did he see in the log? A snake!*

    *So, he started to run fast, fast, fast through the forest.* (fast tap)

*He came to a beautiful meadow filled with flowers and grass. It was a*
*good place to lie down and rest. Ah. Let's stop and rest and feel our*
*hearts beating. Is your heart beating fast or slow?*

*As the fox rested there, he realized it wasn't really a snake after all. It*
*was just a branch. How silly to be afraid. So, he put his hands up high*
*and wiggled them all around.* (hold hands up and wiggle them)

*Then he put them down low and waved them across the grass.* (hold
hands low and wave them back and forth)

*Reach up high.* (reach up)

*And reach down low.* (reach down)

*High* (reach up)

*Low* (reach down)

*High* (reach up)

*Low* (reach down)

*That's how the story goes!*

4. Extend the game by asking the children to pair up and do some
   opposites movements together.

   - Can you and your partner reach up high?
   - Now, reach down low.
   - Can you and your partner do a small movement?
   - Can you and your partner do a big movement?
   - Do a tiny movement.
   - Do a giant movement.
   - Can you and your partner take two big steps together?
   - Now, take two little steps together.

   This can be a wonderful way to excuse children from the circle. Give the
   pairs a challenge, and after they have completed it they can go on to
   the next activity.

## Let's Explore Together

1. Use opposites as your theme for movement activities this week, both
   inside and outside. The classic game of Follow the Leader is probably
   the best for building social-interaction skills as well as motor skills. Try
   on the leader hat, and explain that in this game the children need to
   watch and listen to the leader who is wearing the hat and do what she
   says and does.

2.  Put on recorded music, and invite the children to make a line behind you. Start moving around the room to the music. Focus on opposite movements as you move, and say the words that correspond to the movements. For example you might say, "Big steps!" in a big voice as you take giant steps. Then, say, "Tiny steps," in a small voice and lead them around, making tiny tiptoe steps. Keep changing the opposite movements.

3.  Hand the hat to the next child in line, and invite him to be the leader. Remind him to say and do the movements he wants the others to follow. Give the children short turns as the leader so that everyone gets a chance.

4.  Use the leader hat for the Hokey Pokey, too. The leader can suggest what to put in and out of the circle. This game will give children additional experience with opposite movements and will give them more opportunities to lead.

## Learning Extensions and Building Community

1.  Play Hot and Cold to get the children moving in opposite ways. The children will have to work together to help a friend find something hidden in the room. As the child starts looking, the others can say, "Cold," if she is far away from the object and can say, "Hot," if she is close. It is not as easy as it sounds!

2.  Do not forget Simon Says, too! The leader can wear the hat and give the directions. Try using directions that are opposites, but anything will work.

3.  Take an opposites walk outside. The leader can suggest different movements as the line follows her through the playground.

**SEL SPOTLIGHT**

For young children, it can often be more challenging to be a leader than it can be to follow one. Children sometimes freeze when everyone is looking at them, and suddenly they do not want to participate. Be supportive, and help a nervous child find a movement to share. Once he gets started, he will probably be just fine. But if not, allow him to pass the leader hat to another child.

# Look at Me

"Look at me! Look at me!" How many times do you hear that a day? Young children are at a delightful stage of development where they are thrilled and amazed by the new skills they are mastering. Celebrate this stage of mastery with fun activities that let them use their bodies in many different ways. This is a great activity to do toward the end of the year together. It invites children to think about all they have learned to do with their bodies this year!

**Motor Skills:**

- Large-muscle skills
- Small-muscle skills
- Problem solving

**Social-Emotional Skills:**

- Participating in a group
- Sharing in front of a group
- Learning about the body

**Materials:**

- Baby pictures—yours and theirs!
- Baby dolls and supplies (optional)
- Drawing paper
- Crayons and markers
- Glue sticks
- Chart paper or whiteboard

**Ahead of Time:**

Invite families to send in a baby picture for their child. Explain that it will get used in an art project. It needs to be something they do not mind being used this way.

## Let's Get Involved

1. Start the conversation by showing your own baby picture. Children are fascinated to think about their teacher as a baby. Talk about what you can do now that you could not do then, such as snapping your fingers, clapping, and jumping.

2. Invite the children to reflect on what they can do now that they could not do when they were babies. Ask questions to get them thinking and talking: "Could you jump when you were a baby?" "How did you move?" "What did you do with your hands when you were a baby?" "What can you do with your hands now?"

3. Make a then-and-now chart of their ideas. Write what they could do then in one column and what they can do now in the other column. Add to the chart throughout the weeks.

4. Try adding a fun movement song, sung to the tune of "For He's a Jolly Good Fellow":

*I can wiggle my fingers,*
*I can wiggle my fingers,*
*I can wiggle my fingers,*
*Around and around and around.*

The children can add a movement they can do now that they could not do as a baby. Ask them to suggest a movement and then sing it in the song. Invite everyone to join in!

## Let's Explore Together

1. This movement game can be done with the entire group or in small groups. You know your children best and can choose the appropriate setting for a successful activity. Sing the following lyrics to the tune of "Do You Know the Muffin Man?"

   *Do you know what I can do?*
   *What I can do? What I can do?*
   *Do you know what I can do?*
   *And, can you do it, too?*

2. Explain that you are learning a new movement, too, and you want to share it with them. Perhaps it is something like a funny wave or a finger snap. It can be silly and fun for the children to try with you. Demonstrate the movement as you sing the song.

3. Sing the song through a few times, inviting the children to join in.

4. Invite the children to take turns offering a movement they can do. It can be silly or serious—anything goes! Sing the song together a few times as the children attempt to make the same movements that the leader is making.

5. Expand the song game over time by focusing on different movements. For example, the children can do small hand movements one day and big body movements another. This way they get to experiment with both small- and large-motor skills.

6. Add art. Let the children use their baby pictures to create then-and-now pictures. Each child can glue her baby picture on one side of the drawing paper and can draw a picture of herself now on the other side. Ask the children, "How have you changed? What can you do now that you could not do then?"

## Learning Extensions and Building Community

1. Extend the play into your dramatic-play area. Add baby dolls and supplies, and encourage the children to experiment with the roles of baby and caregiver. Notice the roles children gravitate toward. Does the child like being the baby or the caregiver?

2. Does anyone have a baby at home? If so, ask the parent if she would be willing to bring the baby to school for a visit. The children will be thrilled to meet the baby, and the older sibling will enjoy showing the baby to his friends. If possible, ask the parent to visit with the baby periodically. The children can observe the baby's growth and changes over time.

**SEL SPOTLIGHT**

The early childhood years are the perfect time for children to learn how to share in front of a group. The loving and supportive environment that you create provides a safe place for children to show themselves to others. Remember that some children will be watchers most of the year and may never want to take a turn. Allowing children to play the important role of watcher gives them the support they need to eventually become a doer.

# Dance Party!

Have you ever noticed how much young children love to dance? Just put on music, and they start to move. Creative movement is an important part of physical development, creating the mind-body connection that is essential to brain development. When you ask children to creatively express with their bodies, you foster thinking and expression skills while using small and large muscles. At the same time, you are building social-interaction skills. A win-win-win for everyone!

**Motor Skills:**

- Walking
- Sliding
- Stomping
- Hopping
- Waving
- Creative movement
- Creative problem solving

**Social-Emotional Skills:**

- Moving with confidence
- Moving with a partner
- Learning about the body

**Materials:**

- Recorded music selections from home
- Scarves
- Paper-towel tubes
- Streamers
- Tape
- Crayons and markers

**Ahead of Time:**

Invite families to send in recordings of their favorite music from home. They can send mp3 files via email or send in a CD to share.

## Let's Get Involved

1. Introduce the focus on family music with your own family's favorites. "I have some music from my house I want to share with you. Would you like to hear it? Here is one song I like very much. Listen." Play the selection, and notice if any of the children seem to be familiar with the song.

2. Model moving your body to the music without leaving your seat. You can swing and sway, clap and tap, wave and flap! Invite the children to join you.

3. Play different styles of music, such as lively music that you listen to while cooking dinner and softer music that you listen to at bedtime. Ask the children, "How is the music different? How would you move differently to the music?"

4. Explain that in the next few weeks you are going to invite them to bring in their favorite music from home to share and dance to.

## Let's Explore Together

1. Enjoy this activity in a large open space where the children can freely move without fear of bumping into each other or objects. Tell them that they are going to use the music sent in from home to create their very own dance party.

2. Ask the children to help you set the ground rules for the dance party. Invite them to think about how they can cooperate to be sure everyone has a good time. The rules might include being careful not to bump into someone, staying in the dance space, and listening for directions.

3. Define the dance space by walking around the perimeter so that children know that the dancing only happens in this particular area. This will help solve problems with children getting carried away.

4. Introduce a selection: "This music is from Kenya's family. Let's listen for a bit and see how it makes us want to move. Ready? Let's dance!" Play the music, and encourage the children to explore their bodies in response to the music. Dance with them and model the free expression of movement.

5. Stop the music periodically, and have the children freeze and sit down. Put on a new selection and invite them to listen to how it sounds and feels different from the previous selection. Suggest movements to fit the sound of the music. For example, the children can experiment with sliding, hopping, stomping, and waving to the music. "How does your body want to move to this music? Let's dance!"

6. Add props! Let the children make dancing streamers for the next dance party. Provide paper-towel tubes, streamers, markers, and crayons for creating dancing wands! They can tape streamers to one end of the tube and decorate the tube with markers and crayons. Let the dance party begin again!

7. Consider having a dance party every Friday afternoon. The children will look forward to it and will continue to bring in selections from home. They might even want to dress up for Friday dance parties in their best dancing duds!

## Learning Extensions and Building Community

1.  Extend the game by playing Movement Tag. When you play the music, one child is It and moves around the space with a particular movement. The others copy the movement as they try to keep away from getting tagged by the child who is It. If a child is tagged, she becomes It and does a movement for others to copy. Change the musical selections frequently to inspire different movements.

2.  Ask if someone in the children's families would be willing to come to school to sing and play music for the group. This is a wonderful way to celebrate families and diversity. Perhaps they would be willing for you to record their songs so that children can listen to them in class.

### SEL SPOTLIGHT

Creative movement can be empowering for young children because there is no right or wrong way to move. This allows them to express themselves with confidence in their own choices, knowing that they will not be criticized or corrected.

# Circle around with Friends

Circle games are a classic early childhood device for building physical skills and creating community. With a focus on both movement and friends, these activities are excellent for building the heart and mind of movement.

## Motor Skills:

- Large-muscle skills
- Small-muscle skills
- Directionality

## Social-Emotional Skills:

- Cooperating
- Sharing with friends
- Participating in the group

## Materials:

- Large plastic hoop
- Embroidery hoop
- Large ball of yarn or string
- Ribbons or strips of fabric

## Ahead of Time:

Create a movement ring for circle games. Use a plastic ring such as an embroidery hoop or a plastic container cover with the center cut out. Tie ribbons or strips of fabric to the edges of the ring.

## Let's Get Involved

1. There is something about a circle of children that just inspires creative movement and community, perhaps because all children are seen equally. Welcome the children with a fun fine-muscle movement game that invites them to see their connection to everyone in the circle. Show them the ball of yarn, and explain that they are going to use it to make connections around and across the circle.

2. Hold one end of the yarn and say your name, then roll the ball to someone across the circle. When that child gets the ball, he says his name, holds onto some of the yarn, then rolls the ball to another child. There is really no wrong way to do this. Whatever the children do with the yarn ball, something will be created by the rolling activity.

3. When each child has had a turn to roll the ball, ask the children what the circle looks like to them. "How did it feel to do this together? Do you feel connected to your friends across the circle?"

4. Children now will be ready for a large-muscle circle game. Place a large plastic hoop in the center of the circle to help the children visualize the circular movements. Sing the following lyrics to the tune of "We're Going to Kentucky." This song invites the children to experiment with challenging sideways movements.

*We're going to circle 'round now.* (walk in a circle)
*We're going to circle 'round,* (walk in a circle)
*To slip and slide and slip and slide* (step side-to-side)
*Stepping side-to-side.* (step side-to-side)

*Oh, shimmy to the bottom,* (squat down)
*And shimmy to the top.* (stand up)
*And spin around and spin around* (turn around)
*Until you make a stop!* (freeze)

Play the circle game several times, each time focusing on the sideways movements and enjoying the fun of the stop at the end. You can add zigzag or twirling movements, too.

## Let's Explore Together

1. Invite the children to join you in a movement ring game. Show the children the movement ring you have created. Pass it around so that they can feel its shape and design. Explain that to play the game they are going to walk around the circle with their hands behind their backs.

2. Walk in a circle as you sing the following lyrics to the tune of "Row, Row, Row Your Boat":

*Step, step, step around*
*Step around and sing.*
*Put your hands behind your back.*
*You just might get the ring!*

As the children sing and move, one child is It and walks around the outside of the circle. By the end of the rhyme, the child sneaks the ring into the hands of another child. Sharing at its best!

3. The child who receives the ring is It and suggests a new movement. This time, instead of stepping, the children could march, tiptoe, sidestep, zigzag, or hop. Add the appropriate words to the song as the children repeat the game.

4. Gather the children together after the game to talk about how it felt when they got the ring. Ask how it felt when it was not their turn.

## Learning Extensions and Building Community

1. Let the children stand in a circle and take turns demonstrating a movement for others to copy. Sing the following lyrics to the tune of "Did You Ever See a Lassie?"

   *Did you ever see a good friend,*
   *a good friend, a good friend?*
   *Did you ever see a good friend*
   *Move this way and that?*
   *Go this way and that way*
   *And that way and this way?*
   *Did you ever see a good friend*
   *Move this way and that?*

2. Write out the words and directions for the children's families. These circle games are perfect for playing in the park or the back yard. Invite the whole family to play!

**SEL SPOTLIGHT**
Sharing a movement prop or dance move can be easier for children than sharing a toy. This is because the rules of the game are clear and the expectation for participation is warm and welcoming. These types of circle movement games are excellent practice for sharing more challenging materials and activities.

# Teamwork

The beauty of play with large props such as parachutes or tablecloths is that the activity only works if all the children cooperate to make it happen. This is teamwork at its best.

**Motor Skills:**
- Balance
- Upper-body coordination and strength
- Large muscles
- Rhythmic movement

**Social-Emotional Skills:**
- Working together
- Cooperating
- Taking turns

**Materials:**
- Small parachute or lightweight circular tablecloth
- Playground or beach balls
- Styrofoam packing pieces
- Scarves (optional)
- Large box or box lid

## Let's Get Involved

1. There is nothing like your circle time for enlisting children's help and developing the concept of teamwork. These mini-meetings bring children together to think and problem solve. Start with a brainstorm. Bring out the parachute or tablecloth, and place it inside the circle.

2. Invite the children to suggest what it could be. They may recognize it and give conventional answers. You can extend their thinking by inviting them to imagine how it could be used. There are no wrong answers!

3. Direct their attention to the size of the material. They may notice that it is a very large piece of cloth. Present a teamwork question: "If you wanted to lift it up, could one person do it by herself?" Invite someone to try moving it up and down. "Wow, it is too big! You need friends to help you!"

4. Encourage the children to hold an edge of the cloth and move it up and down. They will soon see that when they work together, they can make the whole fabric move.

5. Add a teamwork chant to the fun. This chant can be used any time you want to call children's attention to the need to work together.

*Teamwork, teamwork,*
*Everybody teamwork.*
*We all work together!*

## Let's Explore Together

1. Gather the children together in a large open space outdoors. Talk about teamwork. Remind them of the chant, and say it together. Ask, "What does *teamwork* mean? The song says, 'We all work together.' What does that mean? How do we do this in our class?" This does not need to be a long discussion. It is more about setting the stage for teamwork activities.

2. Place the parachute or tablecloth in the center of the circle. Explain that they are going to work as a team to use the parachute. Sing the following lyrics to the tune of "Frère Jacques" to pretend to ask the parachute to wake up and play with the group.

   *Are you sleeping?*
   *Are you sleeping?*
   *Parachute?*
   *Parachute?*
   *Time to wake and play now.*
   *Time to wake and play now.*
   *Parachute.*
   *Parachute.*

3. As you continue to sing, encourage the children to help you wake the parachute by shaking it. Ask them to hold the edges and work together to gently shake the parachute. What happens?

4. Ask the children to move a bit faster and watch the parachute start to fill with air and move higher and higher.

5. Ask the children to move slower and watch as the parachute settles back down. "We did it together!"

6. Now that the parachute is awake, you can try more teamwork activities. Place a playground or beach ball in the center of the parachute. Have the children hold the edges with both hands as they try to move the ball back and forth on the parachute. "Can we keep from dropping the ball? Let's work together and see!"

7. Ask one child to hide under the parachute. Sing the following lyrics to the tune of "Frère Jacques."

   *Where is Jeannie?*
   *Where is Jeannie?*
   *Where is she?*

*Where is she?*
*She is under here!*
*She is under here!*
*There she is!*
*There she is!*

Sing for the child as the others work together to raise the parachute and reveal their friend. Some children will not want to hide under the parachute at first but may choose to after they see how the game works and how much fun it is!

## Learning Extensions and Building Community

1. Another day, try a teamwork game with Styrofoam packing pieces. Challenge the team to move the parachute and try to keep the pieces popping into the air. "How long can we keep them moving? How high can they go? Can we pop them all off the parachute?"

2. Brainstorm how many different ways the children can move the parachute. Can they move it up and down? side-to-side? around and around? Try it and see.

3. Extend the play by offering the children scarves to move with. How can they keep them up in the air? How can they fill them with air? What happens when two children work with one scarf?

4. Play a challenging teamwork game with a playground ball and a big box or box lid. Have children stand holding the edges of the box. Place the ball inside. Encourage the children to work together to keep the ball rolling back and forth. "How many times can we get it to touch the opposite side?" Challenge them to keep the ball balanced in the center of the box. Not so easy!

# Jump for Heart

Like a breath of fresh air, studies have shown the direct correlation between movement activities and brain development. Large-motor activities that ask children to move energetically can increase blood flow, which oxygenates the brain. Young children are just learning how to work with a jump rope. Their coordination is such that individual jump roping is quite challenging, but they are often excellent at games with larger ropes and a group of children. Jump roping is a perfect social and motor activity.

**Motor Skills:**

- Large muscles
- Jumping
- Increased heart rate

**Social-Emotional Skills:**

- Supporting each other
- Taking turns
- Participating in a group

**Materials:**

- Two long ropes
- Smaller individual-size jump ropes
- Stethoscope
- Music
- Large plastic hoops (optional)

## Let's Get Involved

1. Start by inviting the children to help you figure something out. Show them a jump rope, and ask them what they think you could do with it in school. Explain that you forgot what it is for, and you need their help in figuring it out! Allow them plenty of time to look at the rope and suggest all the many wonderful ways it can be used. They may or may not suggest jumping with it!

2. Give them a clue by adding a little traditional chant they may know. "I am remembering a rhyme that goes with this. Maybe this will help us."

   *Teddy bear, teddy bear, turn around.*
   *Teddy bear, teddy bear, touch the ground.*
   *Teddy bear, teddy bear, show your shoe.*
   *Teddy bear, teddy bear, that will do.*

3. Invite all the children to stand up and pretend they are holding a jump rope in their hands. Now repeat the rhyme as they jump to the rhythm of the words. At first, it is best for them to jump without doing the actions in the chant. After a few repeats, they can turn around, touch the ground, and so on.

4. When the children are finished jumping, ask them to sit down and put their hands over their hearts. Ask what they feel. "Does your heart feel different than it usually does? Is your heart beating faster?"

Explain that jumping can make their heart beat faster, and this helps them be healthy. After talking about this for a few minutes, ask them to check their heartbeats again. They will notice that their heartbeat is slower now.

## Let's Explore Together

1. After introducing jumping activities with some pretend jumping, children are ready to explore jumping with real ropes. Do this series of jumping games over many days, repeating them frequently so that the children get more and more confident with their jumping skills. Ask the children to remember how their hearts felt after the jumping game. Show them how to touch their wrists or their necks to feel a pulse. This reflects the beating of their hearts. Let them take the pulse of a friend by holding the friend's wrist lightly and feeling the beat.

2. Start small and low with a group movement game called The Water Is Rising. Two children sit on the ground and hold one long rope stretched between them. This is the water. The children gently wiggle the rope on the ground as the other children line up and take turns jumping across the water.

3. After each pass over the water, the children holding the rope raise it slightly and continue to wiggle it. The game will become more and more challenging as the rope gets higher and higher.

4. Encourage the children to support each other with cheers and chants. They can say, "The water is rising! Jump, Keith, jump!"

5. Play the Wide, Wide River game. Ask six children to sit on the floor, three on one side and three on the other. Each pair faces each other and holds a rope close to the floor parallel to the other two ropes to create a "river" of three ropes.

6. Challenge the other children to cross the river in different ways. "Can you jump with both feet?" "Can you hop the river on one foot?" Eventually, let the children raise the ropes a bit higher for children to jump and hop across.

7. Ask the children to check their heart rates again. They can try a pulse point or share a stethoscope if you have one available. How are their hearts beating now?

8. Eventually, introduce individual jump ropes for practice. The children can start by simply stepping over and over their personal ropes. They can place the rope on the ground and jump over it front and back to get

the feel of the rhythm of jumping. This will prepare them for real jumping with a slow beat.

## Learning Extensions and Building Community

1. Make a River of Rope maze outside on the playground. Place several ropes around the playground in a mazelike path. Invite the children to travel the maze by jumping, hopping, and stepping over the ropes. Try putting one rope up high so they have to squeeze under it!
2. Play a jump rope game using the "Red Rover" chant. The children can hold the rope low and gradually raise it as each child gets a turn to jump over.

   *Red Rover, Red Rover,*
   *Let Sarah jump over!*

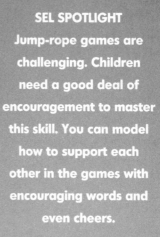

**SEL SPOTLIGHT**
Jump-rope games are challenging. Children need a good deal of encouragement to master this skill. You can model how to support each other in the games with encouraging words and even cheers.

# Finger Dance

Studies have shown a direct correlation between movement activities and brain development. In particular, the fine-motor activities of fingerplays and other hand movements actually create connections in the brain and help support memory development. Let's play with our fingers!

### Motor Skills:

- Small-motor skills
- Rhythmic movement
- Crossing the midline

### Social-Emotional Skills:

- Learning about the body
- Following directions
- Moving with confidence

### Materials:

- Fingerpaint
- Fingerpaint paper
- Drawing paper
- Ink pads
- Poster board
- Markers
- Camera
- Tape or glue

### Ahead of Time:

Make fingerplay charts for your favorite fingerplays. You can use photos of hand motions to illustrate the motions that go with the words.

## Let's Get Involved

1. Welcome the children with your hands. Do not say a word. You can smile and wiggle your finger to invite them to come to the circle. Point to where you want them to sit down. Wave your hand in welcome as they sit down. Put one finger up to your lips to shush everyone for the start of circle.

2. After children have joined you and noticed your movements, start talking. "Welcome everyone! What did you notice about the way we started circle today?" Encourage the children to share what they noticed about your movements. Ask them if they could tell what you were communicating with your hands and fingers.

3. Talk about the many ways our hands can talk for us. How do we use our hands to say hello or goodbye? How do we use our hands to say stop or come here? Offer a movement, and ask the children to guess what you might be communicating.

4. Play a hand-conversation game. Invite the children to turn to a friend and use their hands to talk to each other. They really do not have to say something. It is more important for them to explore the process of using their hands to communicate.

5. Explain that some people use their hands to make signs to communicate with others. They have an entire language for their hands. Introduce a simple American Sign Language sign such as *I love you*: Hold your pinky, thumb, and index finger outstretched as you keep the

two middle fingers folded. To communicate *please*, rub your upper chest in a small circular motion.

## Let's Explore Together

Introduce fingerplays throughout the next few weeks. You can offer a new fingerplay each day, and practice the old ones, too!

1. Share a fun finger-dancing chant with the children. It can be spoken rhythmically or chanted up the scale.

   *One finger, one thumb keep moving* (wiggle a finger and thumb)
   *One finger, one thumb keep moving* (wiggle a finger and thumb)
   *One finger, one thumb keep moving* (wiggle a finger and thumb)
   *To dance the cares away.*

2. Encourage the children to find a partner and do the rhyme again. This time, each pair must touch their fingers and thumbs together as they do the movements. Ask them to reach across their bodies to touch the finger and thumb of their friend's opposite hand. Be prepared for the children to end up giggling together!

3. A similar song and movement game to try is "Johnny Works with One Hammer."

   *Johnny works with one hammer,* (pound one fist on a knee)
   *  one hammer, one hammer.*
   *Johnny works with one hammer.*
   *Then, he works with two.* (hold up two hands)
   *Johnny works with two hammers,* (pound both fists on knees)
   *two hammers, two hammers.*
   *Johnny works with two hammers.*
   *Then, he works with three.* (hold up both hands and one foot)
   *Johnny works with three hammers,* (pound both fists and hop on one
   *  foot)*
   *three hammers, three hammers.*
   *Johnny works with three hammers.*
   *Then, he works with four.* (hold up both hands and jump)

   Keep adding body parts as you repeat the rhyme: Four hammers, pound both fists and jump up and down; five hammers, two fists, both

feet, and nod head. End with "Then he goes to sleep." Let the children drop to the floor! Whew!

4.  Extend the activity by adding fingerpaint! Ask, "How can we paint a fingerplay?" Put out fingerpaint paper and paints, and offer another fingerplay to enact, such as "Down by the River." Encourage the children to use both hands to "swim" through the paint. Encourage them to cross the midline of their bodies as they swim over the dam.

*Down by the river in an itty bitty pool*
*Swam three little fishes and a mommy fishy, too.* (pretend to swim fingers
    through the paint)
*"Swim," said the mommy fishy, "Swim, if you can."*
*So they swam and they swam right over the dam.* (cross arms and
    continue to swim)
*Boop, boop, ditta, datta, witta, wattem, shoo!*
*Boop, boop, ditta, datta, witta, wattem, shoo!*
*Boop, boop, ditta, datta, witta, wattem, shoo!*
*And they swam and they swam all over the dam.*
*Splash!*

## Learning Extensions and Building Community

1.  Introduce simple American Sign Language signs for phrases the children can use in class. You can also add a sign-language alphabet chart for the wall. The children can experiment with signing their names.
2.  Send home a list of your favorite fingerplays so the children can share them with their families. Share some simple American Sign Language signs that the family might enjoy using, too.

**SEL SPOTLIGHT**

**The body is the home for all the skills young children are learning. It is through the body that children learn to regulate their feelings and actions. It is important for children to learn about how their body works because this provides them with a sense of confidence in their abilities. All body activities, large and small, build understanding and confidence.**

# References and Recommended Reading

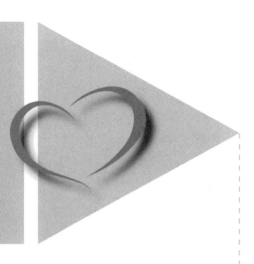

Bodrova, Elena, and Deborah Leong. 2006. *Tools of the Mind: The Vygotskian Approach to Early Childhood Education.* 2nd ed. Upper Saddle River, NJ: Pearson.

Cantin, Rachelle, Trisha Mann, and Alicia Hund. 2012. "Executive Functioning Predicts School Readiness and Success: Implications for Assessment and Intervention." *NASP Communique* 41(4).

Cherry, Clare. 1983. *Please Don't Sit on the Kids: Alternatives to Punitive Discipline.* Belmont, CA: Fearon Teacher Aids.

The Child Mental Health Foundations and Agencies Network. 2000. *A Good Beginning: Sending America's Children to School with Social and Emotional Competence They Need to Succeed.* Bethesda, MD: National Institute of Mental Health.

Denham, Susanne, et al. 2012. "Observing Preschoolers' Social-Emotional Behavior: Structure, Foundations, and Prediction of Early School Success." *Journal of Genetic Psychology* 173(3): 246–278.

Fitzpatrick, Caroline, and Linda Pagani. 2012. "Toddler Working Memory Skills Predict Kindergarten School Readiness." *Intelligence* 40(2): 205–212.

Gopnik, Alison, Andrew Meltzoff, and Patricia Kuhl. 1999. *The Scientist in the Crib: Minds, Brains, and How Children Learn.* New York: William Morrow.

Healy, Jane. 2004. *Your Child's Growing Mind: Brain Development and Learning from Birth to Adolescence.* 3rd ed. New York: Broadway Books.

Jahromi, Laudan, Crystal Bryce, and Jodi Swanson. 2013. "The Importance of Self-Regulation for the School and Peer Engagement of Children with High-Functioning Autism." *Research in Autism Spectrum Disorders* 7(2): 235–246.

Kloo, Daniela, and Josef Perner. 2008. "Training Theory of Mind and Executive Control: A Tool for Improving School Achievement?" *Mind, Brain, and Education* 2(3): 122–127.

Kotulak, Ronald. 2000. "People Skills, Not ABCs, Aid Kindergarteners, Experts Say." *The Chicago Tribune.* September 6.

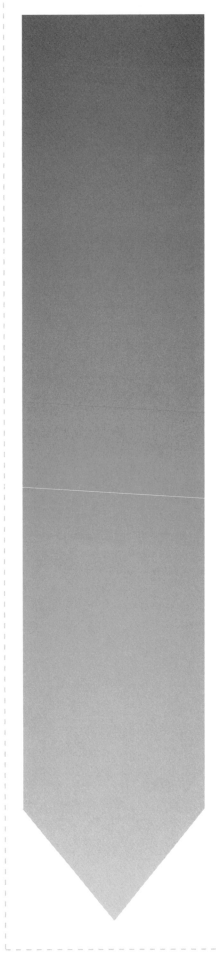

Neuenschwander, Regula, Marianne Rothlisberger, Patrizia Cimeli, and Claudia Roebers. 2012. "How Do Different Aspects of Self-Regulation Predict Successful Adaptation to School?" *Journal of Experimental Child Psychology* 113(3): 353–371.

Shonkoff, Jack, and Deborah Phillips, eds. 2000. *From Neurons to Neighborhoods: The Science of Early Childhood Development.* Washington, DC: National Academies Press.

Shore, Rima. 2003. *Rethinking the Brain: New Insights into Early Development.* Revised ed. New York: Families and Work Institute.

Siegel, Daniel. 2012. *The Developing Mind: How Relationships and the Brain Interact to Shape Who We Are.* 2nd ed. New York: Guilford.

Van der Ven, Sanne, Evelyn Kroesbergen, Jan Boom, and Paul Leseman. 2012. "The Development of Executive Functions and Early Mathematics: A Dynamic Relationship." *British Journal of Educational Psychology* 82(1): 100–119.

# Index